T0035370

MAN AND TECHNOLOGY

How Humanity Thrives in a Changing World

MAN AND TECHNOLOGY

How Humanity Thrives in a Changing World

EDITED BY
KURT ALMQVIST, ALASTAIR BENN
AND MATTIAS HESSÉRUS

BOKFÖRLAGET STOLPE   AXEL AND MARGARET AX:SON JOHNSON FOUNDATION FOR PUBLIC BENEFIT

CONTENTS

INTRODUCTION

The ability to make *tools from tools* distinguishes Mans from other animals. Beavers can fell trees and build sophisticated lodges – and let's not forget the highly complex hives and nests built by bees and ants. But these animals are in a very concrete sense their own tools. However, the technologies that we create are extensions of ourselves. They consist (in some sense of the word) of human tools that enable us to relate to, manage and control our surroundings and our lives.

Chimpanzees use tools to obtain food. But they have not created any machines to do that work for them. 'Does this mean…that technics is actually older than man?' asked Oswald Spengler (1880–1936) in *Man and Technics: A Contribution to a Philosophy of Life*. 'Certainly not', he wrote in answer to his own question. 'There is a vast difference between man and all other animals. The technique of the latter is a generic technique. It is neither inventive nor capable of development. The bee type, ever since it existed, has built its honeycombs exactly as it does now, and will continue to build them so till it is extinct.'[1]

The word *technology* is often used to describe tools, various kinds of equipment, practical skills and knowledge of various technical systems. But technology is present everywhere and in many different contexts. Technology can exist without material tools – for example, predators' techniques to outwit their prey; the knowledge and application of statecraft and diplomacy; and military technology in the form of tactics, strategy and grand strategy.

The chapters in this volume deal with the significance of technology and technique for humans and as an aspect of civilisation. Like *episteme*, the term *techne* refers to knowledge, though of a different sort. We can find numerous uses of these terms from the ancient world, though of course techniques and the phenomena that can be termed *technology* have a past that stretches much further back, into the darkest reaches of prehistory.

We humans have created vast domains of technologies that manifest human abilities. Today they can often seem to be beyond our control. Opposition to and criticism of technology can be seen as equivalent to a more general criticism of civilisation and humankind – a species that seems to have defied Creation, in the view of religious critics, or Nature, in the more secular variant. Lewis Mumford (1895–1990), an influential critic of technological advances, regarded the ominous vision outlined by Marshall McLuhan (1911–1980) as a nightmare, where technology would ultimately take control of progress. In writings such as theirs, human beings are transformed into 'sorcerers' apprentices' who have managed to set phenomenal processes in motion, only to lose control of the results, so that the processes themselves control and steer their creators, who no longer have supremacy over the technology they devised.

This collection of essays is based on the topic planned for the 2020 Engelsberg Seminar. That in-person event had to be cancelled due to the pandemic. Some essays were posted online during 2020 and e2021 on Engelsberg Ideas, the Foundation's digital platform, and alongside newly written texts they are now available in a printed book.

Stockholm 2 May 2022

Kurt Almqvist
President, Axel and Margaret Ax:son Johnson Foundation for Public Benefit

1. Oswald Spengler, *Man and Technics, A Contribution to the Philosophy of Life.* Translated by Charles Francis Atkinson. New York: Alfred A. Knopf, Inc., 1932.

Et in Arcadia Ego (also known as Les Bergers
d'Arcadie or The Arcadian Shepherds),
Nicolas Poussin, 1638.

HOW ARCADIA WAS WON AND LOST AND FOUND AGAIN

Clive Aslet

In the late 1630s, Nicolas Poussin painted a group of Virgilian shepherds inspecting the inscription on a tomb. Wonderingly, they decipher the words 'Et in Arcadia Ego', which loosely translates as 'I am even present in Arcadia.' The first-person singular has generally been taken to mean death, reminding the spectator that even these beautiful, unlettered young rustics will be struck down in the fullness of time. Nearly 400 years later this painting remains relevant, not just to the human condition in general but to the Arcadia of the countryside in particular, and certainly that found in Britain. Untold numbers of people, over many generations, have made parts of it into an idyll, and the process of creating new idylls continues. To many, the countryside is a refuge from the harsh everyday money-grubbing strife of the city. And yet present-day Arcadians cannot escape the external realities that threaten their paradise. Population growth, climate change, a crisis in agriculture, the ugliness of most of the architectural provision for twenty-first-century life…the Garden of Eden famously contained a snake that menaced future happiness, but in the modern day there are many threats to Arcadia. In 1976, the sculptor Ian Hamilton Finlay reworked Poussin's idea in a stone relief, in the National Galleries of Scotland: in the centre of the scene is a tank. Arcadias, the artist appears to be saying, do not arise spontaneously, but are a human construct that must be vigorously defended from outside forces if they are to survive. Not an easy proposition in a democracy whose popular idea of Arcadia is the dating show *Love Island*, filmed on the sun-kissed island of Majorca.

Arcadianism is so deeply rooted in the national psyche that it has created a characteristically British way of seeing landscape and the built environment. A third of Norman England was designated as royal forest – a fiercely protected landscape of glades and groves, set aside for the king's hunting. Medieval magnates not only built hunting lodges but pleasances: hideaways in bucolic situations, where they could escape the hundreds of people that normally surrounded them and hang out with friends. Castles were set amid beautiful lakes. The Elizabethans, having read Virgil and Ovid, plunged into a pastoral world, expressed in poetry, paintings and the imagery of court entertainments. As the country descended into chaos and civil war, Charles I mentally retreated into the pastoralism of court masques. 'Retirement' – the idea that the ideal life could be pursued in the countryside – had been a popular conceit since the age of Ben Jonson, but became obligatory for Royalists who were heavily fined for having fought on the losing side. No doubt similar ideas could be found throughout Europe, but from around 1700 arose a characteristically British movement, when gentlemen competed to turn their parks into three-dimensional evocations of the paintings they had seen on the Grand Tour. Poussin's *Et in Arcadia Ego* and works like it transcended the realm of the ideal and became real, under the hand of the gardener 'Capability' Brown and his followers. This was the aesthetic of 'the pictur-esque', which has been called Britain's great contribution to the visual culture of Europe.

Influenced by the picturesque concept of the sublime, Romantic poets like Wordsworth worshipped nature, in all its rawness, savagery and beauty. Nature was the balm that could assuage the squalor and human misery of the Industrial Revolution. That was the Victorian seer John Ruskin's idea, and it begat another British phenomenon: the Arts and Crafts Movement. Arts and Crafts failed, industry won – but ruralism and nostalgia permeated the British imagination. Although, by a creep-ing, inevitable process, Britain's capital city grew to Brobdingnagian proportions, nearly everything that was distinctively British in music and visual culture in the twentieth century was anti-urban.

There was good reason to fear the city, too. Until the Clean Air Act of 1956, London's notorious smogs, a combination of damp air and coal smoke, blotted out the health-giving sun; the city was black with soot. Slum children grew up with rickets from lack of vitamin D. Families who could afford to decamp went to the new suburbs that ballooned outwards, leaving only a few hedges to recall what the poet John Betjeman called 'our lost Elysium – rural Middlesex'. Betjeman was part of the pushback against urbanisation, supported by aesthetes, traditionalists, ramblers and lovers of country sports. After the Second World War, the Town and Country Planning Acts sought to impose order on both urban and rural development, which had until then been largely unplanned, through a system of controls which required planning permission. They did a better job of protecting the countryside than creating or preserving beauty in cities. Bombed-out and decayed areas of cities were cleared and replaced by high-rise blocks which, supporters claimed, would ultimately provide aesthetic pleasure through contrast and variety – principles of the picturesque. Villages were never subject to these pressures, and open farmland, while drenched in chemicals to kill weeds and pests, was protected as part of a national policy to boost agricultural production. In hindsight, it is possible to see that the most beautiful cities in Europe, such as Paris, are classically planned: they have streets and squares lined with blocks of buildings similar in appearance and height. Still under the spell of the picturesque, Britain resists regularity, prefers the piecemeal; mandates mix and match. London has been strewn with high-rise towers. Ironically, this visual disaster is a fruit of the picturesque movement – the very doctrine that has made Britain so sensitive to, and protective of, the countryside.

Around the year 2000, ruralism – all the rage in the 1980s – lost to the city. In the UK, Manchester, Glasgow and particularly London became the happening places: cool, a magnet for the world's young. Culture – art, theatre, music, dance – was intense. Festivals and street food flourished. Public transport improved. A nation that had previously been thought of as somewhat distant in its personal relations found it liked other people crowding together to watch Pride parades and the New Year's Eve fireworks. So many office workers coming into the centre, so many tourists – their numbers joined by the increasing amounts of people who chose to live in the heart of the city, making the pavements too narrow for the hordes using them. London property prices soared into a stratosphere barely imaginable to those living elsewhere. The ripple effect that traditionally caused country prices to catch up with those in the capital stopped. Britain became two countries: London and everywhere else.

Now, the pendulum could be swinging back. Cosmopolitan London decried Brexit. Who would make its cappuccinos when the Spanish baristas had gone? Wouldn't the great money tree of the City of London be poisoned at the root? Even before such fears could be put to the test, the pandemic hit. London emptied. Village homes that had previously been hanging on the market unsold were snapped up by professionals, escaping London much as Henry VIII had fled the plague. In Second World War parlance, the countryside had a good Covid. Urbanites, confined to taking one walk for exercise a day, looked with envy at the Instagram feed of their country-dwelling friends, who could hold barbecues in the garden. Families with large houses were pleased to see their young return from shared flats in the city. Commuting was put on hold, and it is now questionable whether it will ever resume on the same scale; it is costly both in terms of office space and human wear and tear. Long months confined to the same quarters made homeowners re-evaluate their surroundings, and the end of lockdown was followed by a scramble to move house. This time it is country prices that are up and London properties that don't sell.

Before Covid, office workers trudged to their desks. Now, changes that might have taken a couple of decades to come into effect have been adopted in 18 months. Britain has discovered Zoom. Villages that have been deserted during the day should, in theory, become vibrant again. Shops and pubs should reopen as commuters spend more time at home. More holidays are being spent in the home country. There is perceived virtue in supposedly more natural ways of life, which are theoretically greener, causing less damage to the planet – although the image of a low-impact lifestyle may be belied by the reality; try living in the country-side without a car. Whether or not these trends prove to be permanent, they contribute to a narrative that was already beginning to take hold before the pandemic, the vogue for country chic. Arcadia rocks.

An intimation of this can be seen in Somerset, where The Newt, an 800-acre development of gardens, restaurants, shopping, beekeeping and landscape has become truly an Elysium to visit and relax in – for those who can afford the membership fee. A Roman villa found on the property has been excavated and will become another attraction, together with a full-scale reconstruction of what it might have looked like in its prime. Ten minutes away, the town of Bruton has been colonised by the contemporary art dealers Hauser & Wirth; the art – large, spectacular, international – is displayed in old barns. A restaurant has been created in a former farmyard. These activities are transforming a previously unprosperous part of the countryside, through what might be called 'the Arcadian economy'.

The Newt and Hauser & Wirth fashionably combine stylish modern design – lots of right angles and glass – with traditional stone buildings. The Daylesford farm shop, inspired by Lady Bamford's organic kitchen garden, gives off a similar vibe. Country houses like Chatsworth and

Houghton insert new art into ancient settings – indeed, a new book on the Duke of Devonshire's family seat is called *Chatsworth, Arcadia, Now*, suggesting that Arcadia remains a living place, as it was when Chatsworth was first built around 1700.

But this is not the only vision of Arcadia on offer. In their different ways, the architect Ben Pentreath, the artist Luke Edward Hall, and Matthew Rice, the designer and general manager of the pottery company Emma Bridgewater, offer a more nostalgic vision, in the tradition of the interwar artists Eric Ravilious and Edward Bawden. It is deeply English (and Scottish and Welsh too). It is also easier to access by those who care about what they eat. A generation ago, good restaurants in the countryside were few and far between, and greengrocers did not sell avocados. Gastropubs are now everywhere, and the local food economy has produced an astonishing number of cheesemakers, wineries and purveyors of meat from rare breeds (there are also supermarkets whose shelves bulge with the world's produce, for those who prefer them).

The countryside is now truly Virgilian – a place where the successful, whose money and reputation have been made in cities, can refresh their energies in a rural setting but with the appurtenances of civilisation at hand. Parts of the countryside, I should say. For the description applies to the hilly west of the country rather than the agricultural east – although an outbreak of Arcadianism can be seen along the fashionable North Norfolk coast. Certain parts of the country have done well from it. You only have to look at the immaculate state of some Cotswold villages, whose cottages would have been all but uninhabitable a century ago, to see that it's a source of prosperity.

But remember the snake. Go to the county town of Gloucester, a city with a cathedral, and the picture is altogether bleaker. Here is the other face of the countryside, where increasingly great wealth exists in close but unacknowledged proximity to poverty. As many as 37% of children in some parts of Gloucester are living in poverty. The money that might once have been made here has gone instead to Cheltenham, with its racecourse, literary festival and billion-pound companies. Gloucester has stuck with the countryside's traditional activity of farming and suffered.

By definition, Arcadias do not occur everywhere. They are limited in size and separate from ordinary life. You may even have to close your eyes to see these places of the imagination – and certainly close them to some things that would otherwise destroy the carefully constructed image of a perfect world. The gun of Hamilton Finlay's tank must be kept loaded and ready to fire. Life has become more comfortable and sometimes more beautiful than it was in the mid-1970s when his artwork was made – railway services have improved, mobile phones have replaced telephones in kiosks, old buildings are routinely repaired, not demolished, road verges aren't cut until after No Mow May to help wildflowers. But the threats remain legion.

Let's consider just two of the many complex issues. First, the revolution that is underway in farming. Few Arcadians are directly engaged in agriculture – indeed, the number of people employed in the workforce is tiny and the contribution to Britain's GDP is small. But since farming remains by far the largest land use in the countryside and dictates what, other than housing estates, are allowed to thrive there, it is important to everyone. Recent history has not been good. Nature is on the retreat. There may be more urban foxes, and some reintroductions, such as the red kite, dozens of which routinely fill the sky over the M40, have flourished; but the numbers of songbirds, hedgehogs and wildflowers have plummeted. Now Brexit coincides with the fourth agricultural revolution, whose proponents aim to bring automation and big data into farming – and who knows what's in store? Brexit ended the Common Agricultural Policy, whose incentives encouraged the wrong sort of agriculture for conservation. Precious topsoil washed off into rivers, causing floods – and it was never the farmers who paid to clear up. Bigger and bigger machines needed bigger and bigger fields. Anything that competed with crops was eliminated. Some of the damage was mitigated by environmental stewardship schemes, but they were too patchy to stop the general collapse of some species. When I drove my motorbike from Cambridge to London in the mid-1970s, I had to stop at least once during summer months to wipe my visor clean – it was splattered with insectan body parts. These days, the car windscreen is clear.

Post-Brexit, rural policy can be rethought from first principles. We can fit the countryside for the fast-moving, environmentally conscious twenty-first century, rather than the Continental Europe of the 1950s. The flat eastern half of the UK will produce more, while the hills of the west, which include many of our most beautiful landscapes, will be managed for low-intensity grazing and conservation; rural tourism is already booming, due to Covid.

So picture it. Farming becomes more efficient. Consumers see more fully traceable British food in supermarkets and shops, grown to the best environmental and welfare standards. Nature gets more breathing space. This win-win is made possible by the efficiencies of technology. Gene editing, opposed by the bureaucrats of the EU, offers the prospect of disease-resistant crops that grow better in the northerly climate of Britain. Supersized, red diesel-guzzling tractors and combines will become as outdated as Zeppelins. The future lies with small robotic tractors, operating with GPS to deliver exactly the right amount of nutrients to the soil, with micro precision. Britain has the possibility of growing more of its own food. The gigantic greenhouse development of Thanet Earth, in north-east Kent, is providing supermarkets with many of the salad crops that would otherwise be trundled over in carbon-unfriendly lorries from Holland or Spain.

That is the vision, and Arcadians should embrace it. Modern, in this case, means better. More wildflowers will bloom beside the picnic rug when it is spread on a meadow – and there should be more meadows, which have reduced to a mere 3% of their number since the Second World War. But this glorious future could be bitten by the snake of the post-Brexit free trade agreements Britain is making with the rest of the world. Australian and American farmers want better access to the UK market, and the scale on which they can produce food will undercut the home industry. If agriculture becomes unprofitable, farmers will try to squeeze more out of the land. Goodbye conservation. Expect more solar panels and golf courses.

Secondly, housing. Britain is unlike most other European countries; its rural areas are not depopulating but filling up. The pressure to build more homes in the hope of deflating house prices is huge. The population is expanding rapidly, due largely to immigration. First-generation immigrants tend to live in cities, but their children and grandchildren may have other tastes. Volume encourages housebuilders to construct estates on fields rather than on complicated urban wasteland. Tax breaks should be given to encourage the redevelopment of out-of-town shopping malls now that Jeff Bezos has made them redundant. Low-rise commercial sheds surrounded by acres of car park are not only hideous, but an inefficient way to use precious land. This idea has yet to capture the imagination of government. Instead, ministers seem unable to stem the tide of concrete flowing towards the countryside. Everyone wants their own slice of Arcadia. But if everyone gets one, how much will be left?

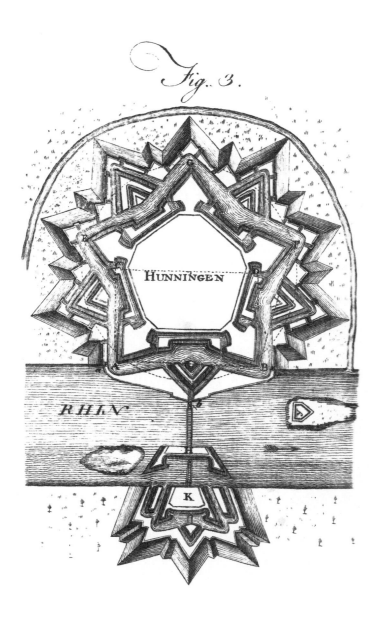

Illustration of Huningue (Hüningen) fortification
designed by Sébastien Le Prestre de Vauban,
unknown date.

ON GUARD: THE CONTEMPORARY SALIENCE OF MILITARY FORTIFICATION

David J. Betz

If asked to picture a castle, most people would imagine a historical artefact, a museum piece, or maybe a fantastical Disney confection. What they would not imagine is a piece of currently relevant military engineering. Nevertheless, in January 2021 it was reported that French forces fighting Islamist rebels in Mali had constructed two new forts, one at Labbezanga, a small port village on the Niger River and the other at Menaka, a town about 200 kilometres away, also near the Niger border. Normally, the expansion of the world's existing stockpile of fortified outposts in far-off dusty places would not be newsworthy. But these Malian forts speak to a vast and growing yet little remarked upon trend – ever-increasing global fortification, both by the military and civil organisations.

Governments at all levels, private companies, communities both large and small, even criminal entities, are all building fortresses of one sort or another at an astonishing pace. The fact is that ours is a physically guarded age as much as any time since the castellated days of yore. Modern life is conducted within concentric layers of fortification. True, a great deal of it is hidden in plain sight, designed to look like something else, and some of it, such as surveillance systems, is intangible, but most of it is tangible – and it is everywhere.

Moreover, fortification today is good business, outstripping in size other major categories of military investment, and growing while others are shrinking.

Mali's two new forts may not be the magical fairy-tale castles of cultural imagination, but they are nevertheless eye-catching, as, in an obvious nod to the seventeenth-century French military engineer Sébastien Le Prestre de Vauban, they are constructed in a 'star fortress' pattern. It's well over two centuries since this form of architecture was at its peak, but our modern guarded age is full of similarly inventive structures and products including barriers, border walls, guard towers and armoured gatehouses.

And not only does a very large fortification market exist, it consists of a huge range of products. To give an indication of scale, the IFSEC Global Directory (a UK-based listing of security sector manufacturers and service providers) currently lists 355 companies selling 'perimeter security' products from all manner of barriers and bollards to blast resistant doors, with a further 709 different companies marketing various surveillance systems to go along with them. The perimeter security business alone is estimated now to be worth $61 billion annually, with the potential to rise to $96.5 billion by 2026. For comparison, the global estimated annual value of armoured vehicle sales, a more obvious military product, was $25.5bn in 2018. This fortification speaks to the globally perceived threat from mass terrorism – and much more besides.

But first, let us begin with forts. The intrinsic durability of star fortresses is such that the global landscape is still littered with their remains, from the Canadian High Arctic, where the Prince of Wales Fort can be found, to the tropics, such as Sri Lanka's Jaffna fort, which was the scene of a 50-day siege as late as 1995, almost 400 years after it was built. In its classic form, this type of fortress is noteworthy for the meticulous geometry of its interlocking bastions and outer works, including ditches (often flooded) and long sloping glacis all designed to maximise the impact of defensive fire while resisting the blows of siege artillery. Often, they remain in more gentle military use today as barracks, headquarters or residences of high officials, but mostly they have blended picturesquely into a becomingly placid semi-urban scene.

It is doubtful, though, that tourists will be flocking to these new Malian fortresses to admire their aesthetic qualities. Indeed, aside from their basic star shape, which is pleasing from the air, they share little else in common with the grand Renaissance gun fortresses – not least because the surface-mounted structures lack the defining thick glacis. That is no surprise; they aren't designed to defeat siege artillery but to act as a base of operations against different sorts of threats. That does not make them unimportant. Indeed, they are worth a closer look, not because of their seemingly antique morphology but because they are fine examples of a military architecture that is incredibly current, widespread, and surprisingly little remarked upon.

The trick is to look at what the fortresses are built from rather than their shape. The latter is essentially an incidental quality, in this case a bit of a fashion statement. The former is quite a bit more interesting. What if

IKEA and Lego combined their respective design philosophies for making furniture and toys in order to make mass-market kits for building life-size forts? You might expect the result would be something of utilitarian design available in a range of standardised, modular and interlocking shapes, flat-packable for easy shipping, durable (and reusable) while also being relatively cheap. The user could combine these pieces in whatever forms their imagination desired.

In open terrain like that of Mali, where there's no extra cost of preparing the already flat ground, engineers can let inspiration run riot and build star shapes if they want; but more regular polygons with adequate towers would do just as well, particularly for very big bases as seen in Britain's Camp Bastion in Helmand, Afghanistan. More congested or contorted landscapes produce smaller forts that trace the terrain in irregular shapes rather like Iron Age hillforts, as at Combat Outpost (COP) Restrepo in the Korengal Valley.

In some cases, such as at gatehouses, which need to limit the potential damage of vehicle-borne bombs, a fortified switchback or serpentine shape that slows vehicles and prevents direct approaches to entrances is called for. The potential combinations are very great, depending on tactical factors such as terrain and the nature of the supposed threat, as well as the primary consideration of cost and the rarer consideration of aesthetics.

One of the most recognisable and interesting products is the HESCO bastion, manufactured by a British company based in Bradford. It is essentially a gabion (a large basket filled with earth and stone), a very old piece of military technology. Think of it as a big building block. In the old days these were constructed out of wicker and used to provide protection from enemy gunfire during sieges.

The modern version invented by British entrepreneur Jimi Heseldon, initially as an anti-erosion barrier (for which it is still in wide civilian use), is made of hinged wire mesh with a sturdy geotextile lining. Easy to ship and to set up, given an adequate supply of local dirt, a handful of soldiers with a front-end loader can stack them into a workable fortress in a few hours. It is a commendable piece of modern design, rather like Mies van der Rohe's famous Barcelona chair – a reinvention of an old and familiar thing in a new and current way.

What HESCO lacks in grandeur it makes up for in utility. Under fire, loose-packed earth has huge damage resistance as opposed to more solid constructions, which often shatter and spall dangerous fragments. In addition to military usage, it is employed heavily in the humanitarian sector, for example as a safe haven for vulnerable aid workers, in industry for the protection of critical infrastructure, such as refineries, and generally as a rapidly deployable perimeter protection system with a multitude of uses.

The forms in which HESCO forts can be built are as varied as the combination of imagination, tactical exigency and cost allows. It is to the 'War on Terror' what the Huey helicopter was to Vietnam – the ever-present backdrop to a million war photos. The scale of civil governmental and NGO use is also noteworthy. For example, according to the latest available accounts of the United Nations Procurement Division, in 2013–14 it purchased around $75 million worth of HESCO gabions, security barriers and prefabricated fortifications.

HESCO is by no means the only significant military engineering product in increasingly wide use. The sector is burgeoning with other reinvented fortification technologies, from portable marching forts to modular armoured guard posts, to an assortment of concrete T-walls (originally a highway safety device) for protection against low-trajectory weapons and blast mitigation. The last are frequently used in base building, but their most remarkable recent employment is in urban counter-insurgency. Repurposed as barriers separating warring neighbourhoods, they are dubbed 'peace walls', and proved highly useful in reducing violence in Baghdad in 2008. Unfortunately, as can be seen in Belfast, where the British started employing them nearly 50 years ago, they tend to become permanent.

For obvious reasons, fortifications are particularly evident in Afghanistan, where every army base, government centre, transport hub and much else besides is girded by walls and ditches, blast barriers, guard towers and armoured gatehouses. The same may be said of practically any contemporary conflict zone. Mogadishu, Somalia, where the fortified 'green zone' around the airport effectively provides an armoured cantonment for international visitors, is a good example too; but looking at Afghanistan alone yields some useful generalisations.

The first is that fortified life is not the exception to the rule of contemporary military affairs but the default experience of war; if not always for the locals, then nearly always for foreign troops, diplomats and other officials. Most troops on operational deployment – 90% or more – never or very rarely leave them. They arrive by air into a fortified cantonment somewhere, perform their duties, and depart the same way they came without ever having left its confines. The cost of a big fortified base is in the hundreds of millions of dollars. Kandahar Airfield, for instance, was a midsize town with a daytime population of 20,000 (dropping to about 12,000 at night when local workers had gone home), with an infamous boardwalk of shops and restaurants at its height in 2010. The US embassy in Kabul was reported to have cost $1.5bn to build and secure.

It would certainly be hard to have missed the fortified quality of contemporary military operations during the recent chaotic withdrawal of NATO from Afghanistan. The backdrops to desperate scenes of people attempting to flee the Taliban via Hamid Karzai International Airport were walls decked with razor wire, sewage-laden moats, and gates loomed over by armoured towers. It is arguable that miasmic debacle did not become a twenty-first-century Alamo, or Dien Bien Phu, though if the Taliban had contested the withdrawal by targeting the vulnerable airfield it could have turned out that way.

On the way to the airport, American diplomats lifting off in helicopters from their embassy compound might have glimpsed the site of the old British Sherpur cantonment a half-mile away. Abandoned after a siege in 1879 during the Second Anglo-Afghan War, it is now a military cemetery, known locally as Kabre Gora, or the 'foreigners' graveyard'. Truly, as Mark Twain quipped, while history rarely repeats itself exactly, it often 'rhymes'.

This suggests another generalisation: the huge continuity in fortification, often remarked upon by soldiers and other visitors. Most fortresses are built on or in the shadow of older ones, for largely the same reasons, and to much the same result. The landscape of the most recent Afghan war was comprised of layer after layer of fortification. Jury-rigged NATO castles were often built around the remains of Soviet fortified outposts, which in turn were heaped on the site of derelict British fortresses, some of which rested on even older ones built by or against invaders ranging from the Mongols to the Macedonian Greeks.

Combat Outpost (COP) Coleman in the eastern Kunar province was built around a nineteenth-century British border fortress, while COP Castle (the hint is in the name) in Helmand province incorporated a twelfth-century castle once besieged by Genghis Khan's army. Near Qalat City in Zabul province, soldiers at two Forward Operating Bases named Langman and Apache, guarding Highway 1 (which runs along the old Silk Road) were overlooked by a fortress built by the army of Alexander the Great. Marines based at Fort Barcha in Garmsir district, Helmand, renamed their decomposing mud-brick outpost 'Castle Greyskull' in a nod to the fictional 1980s *Masters of The Universe* fortress. It had previously been occupied by the Soviets, who extensively tunnelled out and added to a pre-existing fortress of uncertain vintage. A full list would be very long indeed.

Finally, the scale of fortification is also noteworthy. By 2010 it was reported that Afghanistan had 700 fortified bases and outposts, approximately 300 of them held by the Afghan national army and police – all now abandoned or held by the Taliban. Time awaits the arrival of a new imperial adventure, no doubt, to add another layer of strategic stratigraphy.

This impressive number, however, is exceeded by the efforts of neighbouring Pakistan, which was estimated by the end of 2021 to have built (or recommissioned) as many as 1,000 forts and border posts along its border with Afghanistan. These are but one part of a fortified strategic complex that includes approximately 1,500 miles of dual chain link and barbed wire fencing, a ditch measuring 400 miles in length, 14 feet in width and 11 feet in depth, plus an array of cameras and other electronic sensors. The cost of all this was reported to be $500m. The Afghanistan-Pakistan region is impressively heavily fortified – but similar levels of effort are observable elsewhere in the world too.

There has, of course, been a good deal of attention paid to such continuous frontier fortifications since the 2016 US presidential election of Donald Trump on a campaign promise to build (more exactly to extend and reinforce) a wall on the US–Mexico border. The contentious politics on this issue have focused largely on migration policy and not military affairs. There is good reason for that. Some peripheral linear barriers have little or nothing to do with military defence – America's Mexican border is a case in point. Likewise, Europe's anti-migration barriers, which are hardly less extensive than Trump's proposed wall, have had mixed success, though their symbolic power as a rebuke of borderlessness, a central idea of globalisation, is great.

These realities distract, however, from the fact that some of these huge linear barriers are objects of substantial and creative *military* engineering, serving the national security strategy of at least a dozen nation states around the globe today. What has been happening for a few decades, although rapidly hastening in recent years, is fortification on a scale that exceeds by an order of magnitude the famous efforts of the Roman emperor Hadrian in north Britain and rivals that of the Great Wall of China – and nearly all of that in the space of a generation or two.

Perhaps the most well known is Morocco's Western Sahara Wall, often referred to as the 'Sand Wall'. The appellation is not surprising as the vast majority of its 1,600-mile length is of a sand berm and ditch construction, not dissimilar in form from the ancient Offa's Dyke in Britain or the traces of the Roman Limes still detectable across Germany between the Rhine and Danube rivers. It is also, however, somewhat misleading as to the degree of effort and sophistication of its construction. Dotted with relentless regularity every three to five miles along the Sand Wall are forts manned by as many as 100,000 Moroccan soldiers. The gaps, moreover, are covered by high fences in many places, several layers of barbed wire, a range of electronic surveillance devices, and approximately seven million landmines. By any measure this is a serious work of fortification that has occupied the bulk of national military effort for the last 30 years.

It is sometimes said that so vast is the Great Wall of China it is visible from space. Alas, this is untrue. Linear fortifications, while often very long, are relatively thin, and this lack of depth is one reason they tend to lack resilience against high-intensity threats. As it happens, though, the fortification of the border between India and Pakistan can be seen from orbit, at least at night, because approximately two thirds of its 2,000 miles is constantly floodlit – at enormous cost. The 3,000 mile India-Bangladesh border has also been progressively fortified in a multi-decade project first proposed by Prime Minister Indira Gandhi in the early 1980s, a few years before she was assassinated. Although primarily an anti-migration barrier, it is heavily policed – between 2001 and 2010 Indian security forces are estimated to have shot 900 Bangladeshis crossing the frontier. Casualty figures for the most recent decade are not available.

The number of such barriers in the world today varies according to how and what one counts. A few, such as that between South Africa and Mozambique, are rudimentary and effectively now derelict for lack of money, though the perceived need for them has not diminished. Some such as that between Kenya and Somalia are seemingly half-built or mired in delay. The so-called 'European Rampart' on Ukraine's border with Russia, now scheduled for completion in 2025, a decade after works began, is another example; others such as the North and South Korean DMZ are thoroughly militarised to the point of practical impregnability outside of a major war. Indubitably, though, there are a great many of them, and they are found on all continents barring Australia and Antarctica. In recent years, among the largest and most technically sophisticated have been built in the Middle East, *inter alia* by Turkey on its border with Syria, and by Saudi Arabia initially on its border with Iraq and now along the Yemeni border as well.

Walls sometimes excite people and sometimes bore them so that they sink beneath notice, and often they do both at the same time. There is a beguiling simplicity to them – after all, often what we are talking about are literally just piles of dirt. All the same, they carry a symbolic import-ance that increasingly people perceive, perhaps unconsciously, and they hold portentous, even ominous, messages. Ours is supposed to be a 'li-quid' age of global interdependence, digital connectedness, 'frictionless' flows of goods and people, and constant changes no longer bound (or even slowed down) by the resistance of space. Scholars have declared this to be the zeitgeist as far back as the 1960s. 'The world is flat,' is how Thomas Friedman's bestselling book on globalisation once put it, which is to say it is meant to be inimical to the barriers, obstacles and fortresses of more guarded and less open times.

Military fortification, more specifically, is supposed, in the words of Ian Hogg's *Fortress*, a well-regarded history of military defence, to be a 'redundant science' largely out of step generally with the conditions of modern life, and specifically with the dilemmas of modern warfare. The radically lethal firepower disposed by industrial societies leaves scant role for static fortifications, it is said. This is why, in military affairs and politics generally, when someone wishes to describe a thing as hidebound, retrograde and/or doomed to failure they so often invoke the failure of France's Maginot Line against the German blitzkrieg or declaim a 'fort-ress mentality'.

The problem is that this is all wrong. If you pay more attention to what is done, as opposed to what is said, it is apparent that contemporary war-fare is exceedingly positional in character and increasingly fixed around fortified strategic complexes of great size, complexity and engineering ambition – all of which come at significant expense and require not insig-nificant ingenuity. Moreover, the urge to fortify oneself and ones property is not confined to the military sphere.

The increasing fortification of the urban landscape is a gigantic aspect of the global societal response to the perceived threat of mass terrorism. This, along with the massive corporate and government investment in civil infrastructure hardening, especially of transportation and data networks, require a great deal more study, thought and research if we are truly to understand the age we are living in.

El sueño de la razon produce monstruos (The sleep of reason produces monsters), Francisco de Goya, 1799.

PLAYING WITH DEMONS: HOW THOUGHT EXPERIMENTS GUIDE SCIENTIFIC INNOVATION

Jimena Canales

'The epidemic is a demon,' declared President Xi Jinping to the World Health Organisation on 28 January 2020, 'and we cannot let this demon hide.' Within months, on the opposite side of the planet, a nurse despaired about 'an invisible demon' that had killed half of the residents in her nursing home in Connecticut. Within a year, SARS-CoV-2 infected an estimated 240 million people and would take more than 5 million souls worldwide. Descriptions and depictions of the pandemic as 'demonic' and of the horned and minuscule mutant virus as a 'demon' or 'devil' soon became widespread.

How can advanced technological societies fight against what still seems to us demonic? Science is the obvious candidate. It is credited for developing life-saving technologies – ranging from antiseptics, antibiotics and anaesthesia to vaccines – as well as many other innovations that have improved the quality of life for many around the world.

Popularisers of science tend to focus on how the discipline increases our ability to control and predict nature, but those aspects of science that introduce new variables into our universe affect us in more alarming ways. The astronomer and science communicator Carl Sagan is a typical example of a thinker who mostly ignored those uncomfortable aspects of science. Yet even he admitted that in the process of discovery, 'surprises – even some of mythic proportions – are possible, maybe even likely.' Accidental discoveries often beget regret, hand-wringing and soul-searching. How can we conduct research so that discoveries pleasantly surprise us? According to Sagan, the only way forward is forward: 'If we knew beforehand what we'd find, it would be unnecessary to go.'

Five years before the pandemic started, scientists studying bat viruses at the Wuhan Institute of Virology in human cells and in mice were surprised when they created a chimeric mutant that made them sicker. Such an outcome was 'not expected', they said in a paper titled 'A SARS-like cluster of circulating bat coronaviruses shows potential for human emergence'. Like many others, the discovery was a game changer: it showed just how easily new viruses with pandemic potential could be created in a lab. 'The potential to prepare for and mitigate future outbreaks must be weighed against the risk of creating more dangerous pathogens,' they concluded.

This type of laboratory research is now under the microscope, as is the claim that the 2015 discovery was unexpected. A letter sent on 20 October 2021 by the US's National Institute of Health director Lawrence A. Tabak to the House of Representatives reiterated a claim that such research did not qualify as 'gain of function' (the potentially dangerous practice of genetically altering organisms to enhance biological functions) because it was not the project's stated goal. 'As sometimes occurs in science, this was an unexpected result of the research, as opposed to something that the researchers set out to do,' he wrote.

The history of science is full of examples of surprising and accidental discoveries. From the field of physics alone we know that the discovery of magnetic effects using electric currents (Hans Christian Øersted), radioactivity (Henri Becquerel), X-rays (Wilhelm Röntgen), and radio waves (Heinrich Hertz) caught those involved in the research by surprise. Albert Einstein, who made some important contributions to the study of nuclear energy, was caught off guard when he learned that two atomic bombs had destroyed the Japanese cities of Hiroshima and Nagasaki. 'I did not foresee that [nuclear energy] would be released in my time,' he declared. His colleague and expert in quantum mechanics Max Born noted his and others' blind spots when assessing the impact of their research. Reflecting on his own work, he admitted that 'anyone who would have described the technical applications of this knowledge as we have them today would have been laughed at.'

In science, we can expect the unexpected. Such outcomes do not end after the initial discovery has been made – they continue to occur even at enhanced speeds. Soon after the first 'unexpected' discovery of the more lethal mutant coronavirus in the Wuhan lab, other scientists working with chimeric viruses noted that more surprises might be in store: 'Whereas not generally expected to increase pathogenicity, studies that build reagents based on viruses from animal sources cannot exclude the possibility of increased virulence or altered immunogenicity that promote escape from current countermeasures.'

Scientists' open-ended journeys into the unknown are not always entirely undetermined. Ørsted would not have discovered the magnetic effects had he not been working with electric currents; Becquerel would not have found radioactivity had he not been toying with samples of uranium; Röntgen would not have seen X-rays if it were not for the photographic plates he had stashed in a drawer, and so on. As Louis Pasteur soberly reminded us, in science, luck favours the prepared.

Even before scientists start experimenting, their very first speculations about potential areas of future research are not blind. When trails run cold, these experienced practitioners know where it is most profitable to look, what new discoveries might look like, what properties they might possess, and what they might be capable of. Strange beings haunt scientists' imaginations. Often, these are referred to as demons.

The *Oxford English Dictionary* defines demons in science as 'any of various notional entities having special abilities, used in scientific thought experiments...with reference to the particular person associated with the experiment.' Although these demons are no longer found in the old grimoires of magical spells and incantations, such terms regularly appear in journals, such as *Nature* and the *American Journal of Physics*, science magazines, such as *Scientific American*, and even mainstream news outlets, such as *the New York Times*. Publications dealing with these demons are widely celebrated, authored by highly respected thinkers and scientists, and point to key discoveries in areas ranging from thermodynamics to quantum mechanics. Certain demons, as it turns out, cannot be easily exorcised.

The first demon in this tradition is Descartes' demon, named after the renowned thinker known as the founder of modern logic. In one of the classic works of philosophy, *Meditationes de Prima Philosophia* (1641), René Descartes described fearing a creature who could take over his senses and install an alternative reality in front of him. How could he know what was real and what was illusory? To defend himself from the deceptions of this 'evil genius', he laid out the most certain truths he could find. By doing so, he taught us how to advance knowledge by questioning our dearest assumptions about everything and everyone, including social, religious and political authorities. Thanks to him, scepticism and doubt continue to be the most powerful tools of scientific discovery.

Science's demons are, by most accounts, mere figments of our imagination; they are characters in thought experiments that have pedagogical or heuristic value. There is, however, much more to them. These imaginings have led scientists to mimic their astounding supernatural abilities by developing experiments and technologies to understand them. To this day Descartes' demon inspires us to better understand the imperfection of our senses and to push ratiocination to new levels. Yet he also motivates scientists and engineers to improve virtual reality technologies and create deepfakes – actualising the feats of a creature whose possible existence was first imagined in the seventeenth century.

After Descartes conjured the creature that now goes by his name, other demons entered the argot of the laboratory. 'Laplace's demon' is usually listed next. She was named after the statistician Pierre-Simon Laplace, who originally referred to her as 'an intelligence', using a feminine pronoun in the original French (she was only labelled a demon in the 1920s). Her special abilities included knowing everything about everything by being able to calculate the future by extrapolating from initial conditions. Laplace's hypothetical being could calculate the movement of each and every particle in our universe throughout all space and time. All she needed was a sufficiently large brain and knowledge of basic physics:

An intellect which at any given moment knew all of the forces that animate nature and the mutual positions of the beings that compose it, if this intellect were vast enough to submit the data to analysis, could condense into a single formula the movement of the greatest bodies of the universe and that of the lightest atom; for such an intellect nothing could be uncertain and the future just like the past would be present before its eyes.

Although she started off as a product of the French Revolution, she left a mark in history by becoming, in the hands of the nineteenth-century British inventor Charles Babbage, a blueprint for one of the first computers. When Babbage described the 'calculating engine' he was planning on building, he cited Laplace directly. 'Let us imagine a being, invested with such knowledge,' he wrote, explaining to his readers how the superior 'being' described by Laplace had to be powerful but not infinitely so. 'If man enjoyed a larger command over mathematical analysis, his knowledge of these motions would be more extensive,' he wrote, 'but a being possessed of unbounded knowledge of that science, could trace every minutest consequence of that primary impulse.'

'Maxwell's demon' is the most famous of the lot. He was named after James Clerk Maxwell, a Scottish scientist who most historians would rank third in importance after Albert Einstein and Isaac Newton. It first appeared in print in a section of his book *Theory of Heat* (first published in 1871) appropriately titled 'Limitation of the Second Law of Thermodynamics'. 'Before I conclude,' wrote Maxwell towards the end of the section, 'I wish to direct attention to an aspect of the molecular theory which deserves consideration.' It pertained to 'one of the best-established facts' in thermodynamics, the impossibility of producing 'any inequality of temperature or of pressure without the expenditure of work' – a fancy way of saying that perpetual motion machines could never be built. Maxwell then described a possible exception to the law. 'If we conceive a being whose faculties are so sharpened that he can follow every molecule in its course', the law could be circumvented, and scientists might find themselves able to produce work without requisite expenditure. Maxwell went on to describe his being in the way it would be frequently pictured by generations to come, as working within an insulated container divided by a small door that could allow only certain molecules to pass through:

> Now let us suppose that such a vessel is divided into two portions, A and B, by a division in which there is a small hole, and that a being, who can see the individual molecules, opens and closes this hole, so as to allow only the swifter molecules to pass from A to B, and only the slower ones to pass from B to A.

With his delicate movements, this being could 'contradict' the second law nearly effortlessly: 'He will thus, without expenditure of work, raise the temperature of B and lower that of A, in contradiction to the second law of thermodynamics.'

Decades after Maxwell posited such a creature, the renowned French scientist Henri Poincaré saw him under his microscope. By focusing it on tiny particles that jiggled back and forth when floating on liquids – an effect known as Brownian motion – he attributed their seemingly inexhaustible movement to the actions of an operator working behind the scenes at the molecular level. Such zigzagging movements are not uncommon in nature – they have been attributed to the 'random walks' of drunkards and the fluctuations of the stock market. Because it was up to this demon to determine if atoms and molecules were permitted to pass from one place to another, Poincaré baptised him the 'customs officer' of the universe.

One of this creature's essential characteristics was already widely agreed upon by those who studied him: his tiny size reflected inversely on his strength. Like the fish who could eat a whale, a David who could beat Goliath, or the straw that breaks the camel's back, this miniature Katechon can delay the end of the world, stop entropy, put an end to decay, and with a few deft movements make the world run in reverse. Scientists, including Nobel Prize winners Ilya Prigogine and Manfred Eigen, suspected that he was not only responsible for being at the origin of life, but that he kept life going on in the face of adverse circumstances. His disregard for *human* life, however, was frequently noted by myriad investigators.

As interest in the life sciences grew in the post-war period, Maxwell's demon jumped from physics to biology. Microbiologists interested in studying cell reproduction noticed that something very strange inside them allowed them to self-replicate and organise information in a manner that seems to counter all previously known laws of nature. They started to zero in on the role played by DNA and mRNA in viruses and phages (viruses that attack bacteria) and started comparing them to Maxwell's demons.

Laboratories all over the world are still searching for Maxwell's demon. More recently, a relative of his, called Feynman's demon (after the physicist Richard Feynman, who imagined a still-small imp operating at the level of quantum mechanics), was created in a laboratory setting. 'Feynman's Demon has recently been built as a nanoscale Brownian motor,' stated a recent article. 'Maxwell's demon goes quantum' was the title of another. The international scientific press and newspapers covered advances in research with articles titled, among others: 'A demon of a device', 'Maxwell's demon tamed', 'Demonic chemistry', 'Laws of Nature survive attack by Nano Demon', 'Scientists build Maxwell's demon', and 'Maxwell's demon created by Scottish scientists'.

Because of his ability to churn a profit without loss, Maxwell's demon has fascinated businessmen and economists, who have tried to imitate his *modus operandi*. Jaron Lanier, an interdisciplinary research scientist at Microsoft, recently noticed a particular strategy at play in the banking and tech industries that he compared to the actions of Maxwell's demon. 'Finance, and indeed consumer Internet companies and all kinds of other people using giant computers,' he wrote, 'are trying to become Maxwell's demons in an information network.' Who could blame them? 'With big computing and the ability to compute huge correlations with big data [the temptation] becomes irresistible,' he said. The insurance business, for example, depends on such strategies. 'I'm going to let the people who are cheap to insure through the door, and the people who are expensive to insure have to go the other way until I've created this perfect system that's statistically guaranteed to be highly profitable.' Success at one level, however, led to catastrophe at another: 'For yourself you've created this perfect little business, but you've radiated all the risk, basically, to the society at large.' 'And so,' as Lanier explained, 'you're like Maxwell's demon with the little door.'

One aspect of this creature's masterful tactics is central to Jeff Bezos's management strategy at Amazon, the world's largest multinational online retailer and e-services business. In his annual sales letter to shareholders for 2017, he explained that one reason behind its success lay in a particular decision-making strategy where higher-ups manned one-way doors, just as Maxwell's demon was known to do. 'Some decisions are consequential and irreversible or nearly irreversible – one-way doors, and these decisions must be made methodically, carefully, slowly, with great deliberation and consultation.' By thinking about corporate governance in terms of Maxwell's demon's essential implement (one-way doors), Bezos steered his business away from irreversible losses. 'If you walk through and don't like what you see on the other side,' he warned, 'you can't get back to where you were before.' With such caution in mind, he led Amazon to become the fastest company ever to reach a $100 billion valuation.

Science's demons stop being merely hypothetical the moment experiments are created to understand and imitate the actions of a fine and motley crew, a veritable troupe of colourful characters with recognisable proclivities and abilities who challenge the laws of nature. Thus, they leave the laboratory to impact on the world, leaving us at the mercy of a host of modern demons that thrive in the age of reason.

Science advances not just by eliminating falsehoods through trial-and-error testing procedures – it forges ahead by leaps and bounds when researchers imagine things they still do not fully understand. Fighting demons is more pertinent now than it was in the cruel and misguided age of the Spanish Inquisition and witch trials, but it involves more than just following the science – it requires thinking about who, how and where it is leading us.

Derelict and rusting industrial buildings at the
Humberstone Saltpeter Works, Chile, 2015.

THE WORLD THAT SALTPETRE BUILT

John Darlington

In the high, thin air of Chile's Tarapacá region, a northern extension of the Atacama Desert, lies the ghost town of Humberstone. This once thriving place is now a ruined assemblage of twisted tin sheeting, abandoned houses and disappearing roads, overshadowed by mountainous slag heaps and the skeletons of industrial machinery: a Macchu Picchu for the industrial era. And yet Humberstone, alongside many other deserted neighbours, was once at the heart of an industry that transformed towns and cities, dominated economies, changed politics and led to war, reshaping countries in a way that is still felt today. This bleak but beautiful place has left an extraordinary physical legacy that extends well beyond the sight of the Andes and offers a stark lesson in global influence and the inbuilt vulnerability of supply chains.

At the centre of this story is a simple, naturally occurring chemical compound – sodium nitrate ($NaNO_3$), or saltpetre. And Tarapacá's mineral-rich desert pampas, sandwiched between the Andes and the lower Cordillera de la Costa coastal mountains, has the largest deposits of saltpetre in the world. But the raw ingredients of this story are more than the generosity of geology: personalities and nations are firmly fixed in the equation. Scientists, such as Darwin and Humboldt, helped spread the message of saltpetre's potential to the world. A generation of European entrepreneurs made Chile their home: James Thomas North from Leeds came to South America aged 27 as a boiler riveter and went on to become the 'nitrate king', accruing vast personal wealth and political influence; James 'Santiago' Humberstone, a chemical engineer, had the Tarapacá town renamed after him, while the local *pampinos* who worked there created a distinctive cultural identity.

Tarapacá is a deeply inhospitable region, with rainfall that is effectively zero, and an average temperature of 30°C during the day, dropping to 2°C at night. Consequently, Tarapacá's settlement was largely limited to the coast and occasional desert oasis fed by meltwaters. But a chain of events in the late eighteenth and early nineteenth centuries was to draw global attention to this sparsely occupied area. The fuse was lit by Joseph Dombey, a French scientist, who brought back samples of sodium nitrate to Europe after a scientific expedition in 1778. Shortly afterwards, the Napoleonic Wars increased demand for gunpowder – of which saltpetre is the key ingredient. The new-found resources heightened Spain's interest; its South American colonies included saltpetre-rich provinces. By 1812 several companies had been established inland from the coastal port of Iquique to mine saltpetre for the manufacture of gunpowder.

Despite the potential and demand, the industry was slow to take off. The compound commonly used to create gunpowder is ordinary saltpetre, or potassium nitrate. It burns fiercer, at a lower temperature, and is less absorbent than Chilean sodium nitrate. And, while it was possible to convert Chilean saltpetre to ordinary saltpetre, the early industry was constrained by its inefficiency, requiring concentrated ores of over 60% nitrate content, large quantities of fuel and a transport system reliant on mule trains to cross the mountains to the coast.

Charles Darwin, arriving in 1835 on HMS Beagle, commented on the port city of Iquique and a visit to the fledgling saltpetre industry further inland:

> July 12th We anchored in the port of Iquique…The town contains about a thousand inhabitants, and stands on a little plain of sand at the floor of a great wall of rock, 2000 feet in height, here forming the coast…The aspect of the place was most gloomy; the little port, with its few vessels, and small group of wretched houses, seemed overwhelmed and out of all proportion with the rest of the scene.
>
> The inhabitants live like persons on board a ship: every necessary comes from a distance: water is brought in boards from Pisagua, about forty miles northward…In like manner firewood, and of course every article of food, is imported. Very few animals can be maintained in such a place: on the ensuing morning I hired with difficulty, at the price of four pounds sterling, two mules and a guide to take me to the nitrate of soda works. These are at present the support of Iquique…In one year an amount in value of one hundred thousand pounds sterling ,was sent to France and England. It is principally used as a manure and in the manufacture of nitric acid : owing to its deliquescent property it will not serve for gunpowder.

Despite his reservations, Darwin's description was of an industry on the cusp of massive expansion. In 1840, five years after his visit, the Tarapacá area was producing 73,000 tons of saltpetre, which increased to 500,000 by 1870.

The real trigger for the exponential growth of the desert towns was scientific advances made in Europe during the first half of the century, which demonstrated the value of sodium nitrate as a fertiliser. The growing urban populations of industrial nations across the world required greater agricultural productivity, and discoveries by the German scientist Alexander von Humboldt, the German chemist Justus von Liebig and the French chemist Jean-Baptiste Boussingault – all of whom made trips to what was to become Peru – led to a saltpetre boom.

Ironically, the Napoleonic Wars, with their increased demand for gunpowder, also lit the touchpaper for Chilean independence from Spain, officially declared in 1818. Further north, Peru followed in 1821, with Bolivia declaring independence in 1825. The creation of new nation states gave opportunities to foreign adventurers and entrepreneurs. Land was given freely in return for tax receipts, and European investment in the saltpetre industry grew substantially, led by characters such as Englishmen James North, who went on to become a multimillionaire, and engineer and mine manager James Humberstone.

Over the following decades new technologies significantly improved the efficiency of mining. From 1863, the introduction of the Shanks technique transformed the cottage industry witnessed by Darwin into a fully fledged industrial process. Iodine became an important by-product of the sodium nitrate leaching process, with Chile producing over 70% of the world's supply by the end of the century.

That the three young countries ended up going to war was a reflection of the growing importance of saltpetre to the national economies of Chile, Bolivia and Peru. After independence from Spain, Chile and Bolivia reached agreement about their disputed border; an 1866 treaty made provision for both countries to share the tax revenue of mineral exports on either side of the new border – the zona de beneficios mutuos. A further treaty in 1874 handed Bolivia all the tax revenue from the area, but gave Chilean companies fixed rates for a period of 25 years. This worked in Chile's favour, particularly with significant outside investment from Britain, alongside benefits for a growing Chilean population who served as railway builders and labourers to the industry. In 1878, the Bolivian government imposed a backdated increase on the Chilean companies, who refused to pay and were subsequently threatened with confiscation. Bolivia's seizure of the Antofagasta Nitrate and Railway Company in 1879 led to the arrival of 2,000 Chilean troops in the Bolivian city of Antofagasta and the start of La Guerra del Pacifico, also known as the Saltpetre War. Peru was drawn into the conflict when Bolivia called on a secret treaty agreed just six years earlier.

The war lasted until 1883, beginning at sea and culminating in a series of land battles with the Chilean army moving ever further north, through Bolivia's coastal territories and on to Peru's capital, Lima, which fell in January 1881. Peruvian resistance continued until the Treaty of Ancón. Signed on 20 October 1883, the treaty handed Tarapacá and Antofagasta to Chile, and marked a dramatic rewriting of national boundaries that still has repercussions today. Bolivia's loss of its coast, leaving it a land-locked nation, still plays heavily in the country's psyche, and diplomatic relations have been cut off with Chile since 1978.

After the war, the saltpetre industry in Chile reached its zenith. Foreign investment flooded into Tarapacá and Antofagasta, creating a rail infra-structure that significantly reduced transport expenses. The first railway in the region was constructed in 1871, connecting the La Noria works with Iquique, from where boats transported saltpetre to a hungry world; the network expanded to almost 1,800 km by 1905. British involvement also increased – before the war British investors had interests in 13% of Tarapacá's saltpetre industry, rising to 34% after the war, and 70% by 1890.

In 1888, the modernising Chilean president, José Manuel Balmaceda, sought to nationalise the industry, blocking sales of state-owned assets to foreigners. This, combined with Balmaceda's aspirations for a presidential system, led to the Civil War of 1891, in which British commercial interests and the Chilean political class united in rebellion against the president. A rebel junta formed in Iquique, and its army, backed by the saltpetre businesses, overthrew Balmaceda's forces to form a new government. Unsurprisingly, they supported an outward-looking economic policy which encouraged further foreign investment and export. In return, taxes were levied which brought enormous financial gain to the Chilean state, so much so that by 1890, 50% of the country's *total* revenue came from the duty on saltpetre, and it would remain at that level for almost three decades.

Over a century, the towns of the Tarapacá pampas grew from small industrial villages to large company-managed settlements. In a desert landscape previously devoid of all but the occasional passing human, new towns sprang up, with all the accoutrements of modest civilisation. Humberstone was founded initially in 1862 as La Palma by the Peruvian Nitrate Company, while Santa Laura, less than two kilometres away, was constructed ten years later. The two operations were to become one of the largest works in the Tarapacá, and home to nearly 3,500 residents.

Architecturally, the attributes of these new towns are fascinating. Humberstone is built on a grid plan around a central square, echoing a uniformity commonplace among quickly formed towns across the world. The town's grid of ten-by-six blocks – big, but still a quarter of the size of the tailings mound – was largely made up of accommodation for workers and their families. Constructed in Douglas fir, with stuccoed walls and corrugated zinc roofs, there was a strict hierarchy of buildings reminiscent of Victorian town planning in places such as Lancashire's mill towns. 'Bachelors' lived in their own 4 × 3.5m rooms in barrack blocks with shared bathrooms, while families had small five-room terraced houses that included a front garden and a back yard. Semi-detached accommodation marked a step up the hierarchy for married employees, while the managers had a block of grander houses in one of the smaller public squares, each entered by an arcaded porch and finished with decorative touches.

A town needs services, particularly when the nearest alternatives would require an arid 45-mile trip to the coast. Physical sustenance could be found in the canteen, central market and general store, while the spiritual equivalent was served by a chapel, cinema and theatre. Those seeking more exercise could enjoy basketball, tennis, swimming, pitch-and-toss or football, and the town's children had a school, nursery and scout centre. A hotel and social club looked after guests and locals respectively. Public squares, a bandstand and administrative buildings completed the ensemble.

Given the available resources and desert location, the architecture was simple and functional: the majority of materials, such as the Douglas fir that framed most buildings, had to be imported and brought from the coast. But there were architectural flourishes in adapting to the harsh environment, in particular verandas and covered walkways to afford protection from the sun. And the towns were characterised by distinctive building materials, such as calamine zinc and a 'Pampa cement', the latter made from the saltpetre tailings, alongside examples of extreme upcycling – the swimming pool was made from the recycled iron hull of a boat shipwrecked off Iquique.

At a glance the facilities appeared comprehensive, but the reality of life in a company town varied depending upon status and wealth. The owners, for the large part British, visited from their luxurious homes in the coastal cities. Managers benefited from relatively spacious housing and the range of facilities on offer, while the *pampinos* workers, predominantly men, led hard, dangerous lives. The workers would arrive either from the coast or from the Andes, tempted by the promise of riches, to be equipped, clothed and accommodated by the mining company. Payment was by token, only spendable in the company shop, which made a healthy profit, leaving most workers tied to the place and without the support of a distant family. Corporal punishment by the company administrators, combined with a lack of regulations to protect workers, often led to unrest and brutal repression. It is out of these conditions that the Chilean labour movement grew, firstly through mutual societies and later as unions.

But the most dramatic impact of the desert industry was not felt in places such as Humberstone, but in Chile as a whole. The sheer scale of wealth brought in by saltpetre extended to every area of life. First it was the state that grew: administrators, defence, education and transport infrastructure. The wealth coming into the country was evident in the growth of ports such as Iquique, home to 11 different shipping companies transporting saltpetre across the globe and returning laden with British coal and textiles. The other ports of Antofagasta, Mejillones, Taltal and Pisagua saw a similar expansion, as did its capital Santiago. Chile could not only afford new architecture, but embraced European architectural styles; this was in part aspirational, and partly a reflection of the taste of the expatriates who made Chile their home.

In Santiago saltpetre wealth paid for new law courts, the central post office, the National Library, the Museo Nacional de Bellas Artes, and the remodelling of important churches. The central Alameda railway station belongs to this period, designed by Gustave Eiffel in 1897. Valparaiso, Chile's principal port city, was home to affluent alcoves of British and French expatriates who lived in neighbourhoods with more in common with European communities than local ones. It is little surprise that Valparaiso Wanderers, founded in 1892, is the oldest football club in Latin America – and that their fierce rivals are Everton de Viña del Mar, located just across the bay – each founded by expatriate Britons.

The German response was to invest in science, a strategy that bore fruit when chemists Fritz Haber and Carl Bosch developed a commercially viable means of synthesising nitrate from ammonia in 1913. With no access to the saltpetre fields, German home production increased significantly, overtaking that of Chile by the early 1930s. The impact in Chile was dramatic and, despite the development of more efficient systems of saltpetre production and failed attempts to nationalise the industry, the desert economy collapsed over the course of two decades. By 1950, Chilean nitrate accounted for just 15% of global nitrate production, compared to around 80% during the 1890s. In the 1990s, one hundred years after its peak, the country accounted for just 0.1% of the world's market share.

The impact in the Atacama was abandonment and a return to the desert. Thousands of workers moved to Santiago and southern Chile to find employment, and the mining towns were abandoned, their structures sold, leaving only the tailings mounds as evidence of a once global industry. Humberstone and Santa Clara closed in 1958 and 1960 respectively. Together, they are now a World Heritage Site.

For Chile, the loss was devastating. The League of Nations declared it to be the country most affected by the Great Depression (1929–32), and it took a decade to wean the economy off the easy tax receipts from saltpetre, which distracted from alternative strategies for growth.

Beware the paradox of plenty: the Midas touch, in which geographical locations are blessed with geological abundance, can harbour disaster after short-term gain. This is especially true of communities with a single *raison d'être*, where success and failure are far more fickle than in long-lived places with diverse economic foundations. And it happens throughout history and across the world: the hunt for gold, silver, diamonds or other metals led to the short-lived explosion of mining towns in America, Australia and Namibia, each abandoned once supplies were depleted and newer, more profitable sources took over.

And what of the future? Some of the petrostates of West Asia have seen the writing on the wall and are seeking to diversify their economies, but oil dependence, like that of saltpetre, is a difficult habit to kick. With a tiny public sector, political rigidity and a reluctance to embrace social and economic change, one wonders: will the oil towns of Ahmadi, Awali and Dhahran eventually mirror those of Humberstone and the desert towns of the Atacama?

Illustration from *The Birds of America*,
Robert Havell Jr after John James Audubon, 1838.

NATURE THROUGH THE EYES OF TWO VICTORIANS: A BIRDWATCHER AND HIS BIG-GAME-HUNTING BROTHER

Maria Golia

The world is full of birds, over 10,000 species, more than twice the number of mammal species – they outnumber humans by about 30 to one. A close, convivial, but wild neighbour, they're among nature's most forthcoming representatives, and our interactions with birds shed light on our rapport with both nature and ourselves. It's unsurprising that birdwatching experienced a revival during the Covid pandemic. Whether from an apartment window, a back garden or park, it offered a socially distanced chance to curatively connect with the outdoors. That birds are virtually everywhere makes it easy; there are even phone apps that help identify them by appearance, calls and songs. Spotting and naming birds, getting to know those in one's vicinity, is a gratifying hobby, but to see birds, as opposed to simply watching them, to decipher their behaviour and assign it meaning in the grand, evolutionary scheme of things, is a mission reserved for the intrepid few.

James Bond was an ornithologist. Author Ian Fleming, an amateur birdwatcher, read one of Bond's books, liked the sound of his name, and a spy was born. Nor was it a stretch to name a spy after an ornithologist, since both professions require exceptional alertness and observation skills, not to mention a degree of stealth. Some of the most instructive and ecstatic birdwatchers were British, foremost among them Edmund Selous (1857–1934), whose braving of the elements, zen patience and meticulous note-taking helped advance Darwin's theory of evolution and lay the foundations of ethology, the biological study of animal behaviour that coalesced in the years following his death.

Secure in the exactitude of his observations and proud of his exalted prose, Selous's hermetic, tetchy temperament did not endear him to his contemporaries, nor did his proto-feminist ideas regarding sexual selection. He hated killing and taxidermy, twin tools of the naturalist's trade, calling zoologists 'thanatologists' and natural history museums 'morgues'. But his greatest antagonist was closer to home, his older brother Fred

(1851–1917), a celebrated big-game hunter and sought-after lecturer. Fred had authored four popular accounts of his African adventures by the time Edmund published the first of several books about bird behaviour, where his disdain for hunting (but never Fred) was freely expressed. Both brothers were exemplary Victorians who professed a love of nature; one watched and recorded, the other took aim and fired (ivory tusks were profitable). Between the two, the ambivalence characterising human behaviour towards nature could not be more starkly portrayed.

Our fascination with birds goes way back. The ancient Egyptians adored and worshipped them, but also hunted and bred birds in captivity for food, mummifying millions as votive offerings to the bird-headed gods of wisdom and kingship. Although Tutankhamun had an ostrich hand-fan, feathers were not a favoured ornament; the Egyptian elite preferred gold. The Aztecs liked both, and by 1521 conquistador Hernán Cortés brought their feathered costumes to his patron Charles V, whetting an appetite among Renaissance noblemen for ostrich headgear worthy of a Las Vegas showgirl. Marie Antoinette's brother Joseph called her 'featherhead' for introducing towering plumed headdresses to the ladies of the court. But it wasn't until the 1860s that a full-blown fashion for bird hats hatched in Europe and migrated forthwith to North America. As always, upper-class women were the trendsetters, but during the 60-year reign of the bird hat, feathers became *de rigeur* for women of every background, even if they were only from humble chickens.

Entire birds were mounted in diorama-like arrangements perched atop women's elaborately coiffed heads. Some hats incorporated nests and fledglings; others had birds poised with wings outspread, as if about to take flight. Their appeal lay in appropriating natural beauty to enhance that of the wearer, while expressing a paradoxical appreciation for nature's creations. Birds worked for women as both a symbol and accessory, with motherly connotations and their attention-grabbing appearance. In 1886, ornithologist Frank Chapman hat-watched while walking from his office in uptown Manhattan down to 14th Street, noting 37 bird species along the way. That year, the American Ornithologists' Union (est. 1883) estimated that the hat industry cost the lives of five million birds in North America alone; at the turn of the century, conservationists placed the figure at 200 million.

Domestic and imported birds were culled, some almost to extinction. Hats featuring clusters of feathers (called 'aigrettes' or 'ospreys') were popular, particularly those of the suddenly endangered egret, a member of the fish-catching heron family that was hunted in the Florida Everglades. Its feathers, wrote Edmund Selous, were 'pure shining white…soft as silk' and stiff enough to stand: 'Imagine a little fountain of ivory threads all shooting up together in the air.' The rarer the bird, the better the hat, and the more status conferred on its wearer. Prized for the colour and diversity of their plumage, varieties of birds of paradise were imported from New Guinea and Indonesia by their tens of thousands. The rising death toll eventually ruffled some women's feathers, sparking an ethics debate that became the *raison d'être* behind the founding of the Audubon Society (1886, US) and the Royal Society for the Protection of Birds (1889, UK), both driven by women.

The debate opened on the pages of *Harper's Bazaar*, where bird hats were advertised as must-have fashions for the magazine's upscale women readers. In an article entitled 'The slaughter of the innocents' (1875), Mary Thatcher wrote that while some cultures assigned religious meaning to feather-wearing, here it was only a misplaced vanity. The cruelty of bird wear probably never crossed women's minds; if it had, their 'tender hearts' would intervene, so Thatcher described the plight of birds: how farmers killed them even though they helped control insects, and how the growth of cities infringed on their territory. Nor should we think that birds were created solely for our use and pleasure, Thatcher warned, calling this notion 'a doctrine unworthy of Christendom', even though, according to Genesis 1:28, man's dominion over nature is literally gospel.

Other women followed Thatcher's lead, authoring popular books in a naturalist vein, advocating bird protection. The bird hat debate brought the novel idea of environmental conservation to the fore of civic consciousness, and laws were eventually passed. The Lacey Act of 1900 attached a hefty fine to the interstate commerce of birds. The 1913 Federal Tariff Act placed restrictions on importing and selling feathers, and in 1918, the US Congress passed the Migratory Bird Treaty Act banning feather imports from abroad altogether, and setting a precedent for the Endangered Species Act of 1973. Despite laws, opprobrium and a decline in the trend owing to shorter, symmetrical haircuts calling for more streamlined, 'modern' headwear, bird hats still found wearers in the 1940s. Edmund Selous joined the fray in 1901, taking a fresh approach. Having observed women's behaviour as closely as birds', and concluding that fashion victims heed only their most cherished influencers, he directed *Beautiful Birds* (1901) at children, seeding lavish descriptions of avian marvels with pleas that they make their mothers boycott the bird hat. 'Never, Never leave off asking her!' Selous said.

While writing diatribes for kids with one hand, Selous was doing science with the other, compiling data regarding the behaviour of a variety of species of birds, some individuals of which he watched throughout their years-long lifetimes. His mother, Ann Sherborn, awakened his interest in nature as he grew up in the family house his father built on Gloucester Road, Regent's Park, in London, an area that was then predominantly open fields. His father's third wife and 20 years his junior, Ann possessed a 'deep inborn love of the beauties of Nature' and was 'exceptionally thoughtful and broad minded', her son wrote. Edmund's father, Frederick Sr (1802–1892), was a self-made man, chairman of the London Stock Exchange Committee, a prize-winning chess player, clarinettist and 'witty talker' with a remarkable memory and turn of phrase. In his autobiographical notes, Frederick Sr said that as a seven-year-old schoolboy, 'I was so strong and so hungry that I frequently carried some of the biggest boys around the playground (which was a large one) for an extra slice of bread and butter.'

Edmund was a sickly child, but his brother Fred Jr inherited their father's hearty constitution. While Selous *père* disapproved of sports, Fred excelled at them. Known for his daredevil pranks at boarding school, he was frequently in hot water owing to his poaching of small game and egg collecting, a Victorian pastime of stalking and robbing nests during the brooding season. As a child, reading books by his heroes, missionary explorer David Livingstone and others about lion-hunting in Africa, Fred began to dream, sleeping on his bedroom floor in winter with the window open, to prime himself for nights out on the veld. In 1867, aged 16, Fred's physicality and presence of mind saved his life during a horrific Regent's Park ice skating tragedy when a frozen pond cracked and 41 people drowned. He stayed calm, distributing his weight evenly on a piece of ice, moving from one piece to the next until he reached safety. It was his first brush with death; more awaited in Africa.

A celebrity at 30, Fred's exploits inspired H. Rider Haggard's action hero, Allan Quatermain. On meeting him, people were often surprised he wasn't a bigger man: he was short, trim and athletic, with sun-bleached hair and eyes an uncannily pale shade of blue-grey. The press dubbed him 'the mighty Nimrod', referencing Noah's great-grandson, a king of

Mesopotamia and 'mighty hunter before the lord', a moniker he found embarrassing and which was probably not mentioned at the dinner table on his rare visits home. Fred was a seasoned hunter and explorer by the time Edmund visited him in Africa during 1882–1884, travelling from the south to the interior (present-day Zimbabwe), up the Zambezi River to Victoria Falls, but not always in his brother's company. The record of their time together is scant, suggesting that fraternal bonding was not one of its outcomes; the two corresponded little in later life.

The family never punished Fred for becoming an elephant hunter instead of a doctor or banker. His father financed his first African voyage in 1870, but his profession was at least a source of distress. Fred once described both Edmund and their younger sister Ann as 'melancholic', in other words, boring. They expressed their sentiments about their famous brother by contrasting him with their father, 'a civilised man and a Londoner'. Ann said that 'in character, interests and tastes' they were quite different, while admitting Fred possessed their father's 'strength of purpose, energy, and will to succeed'. Edmund thought that 'nothing at all of [Father] was in my brother's life and being.'

In Edmund's Darwinian appraisal, Fred Jr inherited his 'love of truth and country' from both parents, but the 'call of the wild' that drew him to Africa came from his mother's ancestors, the Scottish Bruces of Clackmannan, a clan of warring kingmakers, and some generations later, James 'the Abyssinian' Bruce (1730–94), who explored portions of North Africa and Ethiopia. Lineage aside, as Edmund tells it, Fred also had little in common with his mother, noting her 'great feeling for and interest in both plant and animal *life*'. He underlined that word, because 'killing was quite another thing for her, and her whole soul shrank from it.' This was as good as saying his brother had no great claim on their mother's affections, whereas Edmund shared all that she held most dear. His devotion to birdwatching and ceaseless condemnation of hunting were expressions of filial love.

The only way to understand birds or any animal, Edmund maintained, was to observe their every foible in the field, on their turf, an attitude that made him unpopular with institution-bound zoologists. 'The real naturalist should be a Boswell, and every creature should be, for him, a Dr Johnson,' he wrote. 'He should think of nothing but his hero's doings.' Edmund followed in the footsteps of Reverend Gilbert White, author of *The Natural History and Antiquities of Selborne (1789)*, sharing White's opinion that knowledge is best obtained by seeing and listening. On his intensive explorations of his village environs White identified three species of willow wren by their calls, and described a nightjar killing an insect, down to the use of 'its middle toe, which is curiously furnished with a serrated claw'. Out rambling, White traded stories with his parishioners about their experience of their surroundings. His book's popularity, running to several hundred editions and still in print, both reflected and promoted a cultural attitude towards nature, combining admiration, inquisitiveness, the ability to watch, learn, and delight in these (morally gratifying) things, while adding some pertinent observations to the record.

Reading White, a young Darwin wondered why 'every gentleman did not become an ornithologist', though most of his contemporaries preferred shooting birds to watching them. Edmund Selous confessed he too had followed this gentlemanly tradition, but the true naturalist, he believed, 'should love a beast and hate a gun'. Any dilettante could shoot, but birdwatching took steely commitment. Selous described the hours-long midnight treks over rough terrain to reach birds' mating grounds in time for the show; fighting cramp while crouched in a mud-hollowed hide, the 'wretchedness, cold and discomfort', the rain and wind that coincided with the mating season and impeded his observations. Nor were birds always watchable, meaning interminable waiting, often to no avail. Telling birds of the same species apart required an almost occult concentration, not least owing to 'the very different spirit [at times] shown by the same bird'. He cultivated stillness, discernment and the fastidiousness to write everything down in real time, while bundled in 'a thick motor suit, warm underclothing, woolen face-protector, sheepskin gloves, two Scotch plaids and a Shetland-shawl comforter'. Along with the agonies came the ecstasy of immersion in his surroundings, near to the point of becoming what he watched. Of the arctic skua, a seabird he studied down to the coloured inside of its mouth, he wrote, 'Oh that cry, that wild, wild cry, that music of the winds, the clouds, the drifting rain and mist – like them, as free as them, voicing their freedom, making their spirit articulate.'

No contemporary naturalist did more than Edmund Selous to advance the theory of sexual selection detailed by Darwin in his *Descent of Man and Selection in Relation to Sex (1871)*. Selous verified, elaborated and sometimes corrected Darwin's observations about mating rituals, where the male performed to win the female's favour, 'like rustics courting at a fair'.

But the idea of female choice, even in animals, did not sit well with his colleagues, so Darwin soft-pedalled, suggesting that females were not really choosing, only naturally more attracted to 'the most beautiful, melodious or gallant males'. Selous was instead adamant about female choice, perhaps because he had a stake in it, since he and his brother Fred fell for the same girl, Fanny Maxwell (1863–1955).

Daughter of a popular novelist, Mary Elizabeth Braddon, and her wealthy publisher, Fanny later admitted she found Fred more attractive, but she chose Edmund, and her decision seems to have informed her husband's studies. When they married in 1886, Edmund had a law degree from Pembroke College, Cambridge. A fast-growing family (a son in 1887, twin girls in 1892) may have prompted the move from London to Suffolk in 1898, but it also marked a change in direction. Edmund now birdwatched full-time, relying on a small trust and the proceeds of his writing. His first paper, 'An Observational Diary of the Habits of Nightjars, Mostly of a Sitting Pair: Notes Taken at Time and on Spot' appeared in 1889 in the *Zoologist,* a journal that encouraged entries in bionomics, 'the study of activities and mental states of living animals'. This suited Selous, who investigated birds like a private eye:

June 22nd, 1898: Crawled up behind a small elder bush some three paces from where a Nightjar had laid her eggs. When nearly there, the bird flew down, not on the nest but close to it. Shortly afterwards, the other bird flew down beside it and immediately I heard a very low and subdued 'churr', expressive of quiet contentment.

British bird-writing had an enthusiastic readership. The widely-distributed *Saturday Review* praised the paper in an article about a new edition of Reverend White's *Natural History of Selborne*, saying Selous had surpassed him in describing bird behaviour. Birds offered an open window into nature's workings, and people wanted to hear about their private lives. At a time of seemingly limitless imperial expansion into foreign lands, coupled with industry's upending of long-established homely routines, it was as if by understanding birds, people might better know themselves; watching or reading about them was a kind of introspective therapy. Reviewing Selous's *Bird Watching*, Warde Fowler, an Oxford don and author of *A Year with Birds* (1886), said it made him feel 'as if I were beginning life again'.

Selous was not writing about birds to entertain. Having observed a variety of species, he delivered evidence for Darwin's theory that males sang and danced to please females, while clarifying the role of male fighting as a courtship behaviour. The female not only took a lively interest, but would intercede on her chosen one's behalf, attacking other contenders. Not all fights were, however, designed for a female audience. Selous explained how Darwin had mistaken the blackcock's 'war-dance' as a courtship display, when it was instead a male-oriented affair that he speculated arose from two prominent and conflicting features of bird nature, 'bellicosity and timidity'. According to Selous, if a bird was threatened, he was not necessarily compelled to fight to assert his position. 'Still, wishing to fight but not daring to would produce mental discomfort, for which some relief must be found.' Selous insightfully described the war dance as a 'substitute for battle', a form of ritualised aggression later identified in other animals, a means of working out rivalries and establishing hierarchies without sacrificing lives.

Watching ruffs compete for female attention, Selous saw that each male had a place in the mating grounds (lek) that when trespassed upon caused a fight, and those that fought hardest got the females (reeves). But in another part of the lek, Selous watched two ruffs procure mates more pacifically owing to their distinctive colouring, winning on looks. Either way, Selous affirmed, the reeves 'take the initiative throughout, and are the true masters of the situation'. As for the blackcock hen's response to male courtship displays, 'one may correctly describe her as fascinated'. Although she fought any female who vied for her chosen male, she played surprisingly hard to get, '[resisting] the charm of the cock's allurements, though exhibiting every sign of being strongly impressed', a behaviour that Selous found 'delicate' and 'human-seeming'.

Selous thought Darwin would be 'triumphantly and most strikingly vindicated' when field data overcame 'denial from the chair', a dig at lettered peers who hadn't observed sexual selection first-hand, instead '[issuing] bulls' from their museums, 'mausoleums whose outmoded theories bore no relation to what actually occurred in nature'. Selous had no zoological degree, and the generous funding assigned to the study of dead versus living birds angered him. When editors wanted to pare down his verbatim field notes, Selous took it personally, accusing them of 'hacking' and 'mangling'. Classified as an amateur despite his achievements, the sharpness of his critique betrayed resentment and undermined the legitimacy of his arguments.

In describing his antithetical brother, Edmund wrote that Fred possessed 'a settled determination that, in its calm unobtrusive force… had in it something elemental'. In other words, he was stubborn as a mule. But so was Edmund, in his resistance to ideas and interactions that might have furthered his work. He eschewed bird banding to facilitate the tracking of individual birds, feeling it his duty to learn to see what the bird saw in distinguishing its fellows. 'Everything should be new to you,' he wrote, 'there should be no such thing as a fact until you have discovered it.' Uncompromising and underappreciated, Selous withdrew, rarely communicating with other naturalists, a position that nonetheless granted an advantage. As an outsider he had the distance to see the academic mainstream with a clarity insiders lacked, and to recognise both the human bias that derailed its thinking and the societal norms behind it.

However suggestive the proofs Selous presented for female choice, they were deemed largely unacceptable, ostensibly owing to expectations that courting birds should behave like humans with respect to male dominance. But Selous knew the real reason his contemporaries had problems with sexual selection was that birds did indeed behave like humans, only in ways that made them uncomfortable: females were not meek, males not in control. 'Why, in fact, should it not be with birds as it is with men and women?' he demanded. Not only did humans make wrong assumptions about animal courtship, they misunderstood their own, and since men's voices were the loudest, they perpetuated their misconceptions. Despite all evidence to the contrary, Selous wrote with some pique:

We have the prevailing idea that (even in a civilised state of things) it is the man…who advances and woman who retires…The reason is probably that the actions of man are of a more downright nature, and easier to observe and follow than those of woman…and that it is man, mostly, and not woman, who has given his opinion on this and other matters, through the most authoritative channels – for it is man who, by virtue of his intellect and his selfishness, holds the chief place of authority.

In detailing the secret lives of birds, Selous revealed the fault lines of patriarchal society, a thankless task. Yet his ideas resonated with members of the younger scientific generation, including Julian Huxley (1887–1975), whose reading of *Bird Watching* inspired his field studies. One of Huxley's papers essentially iterated Selous's findings concerning sexual selection in the redshank. Although he spent far less time in the field than Selous on his path to becoming a pioneering evolutionary biologist,

Huxley affirmed the value of his observations and ideas, helping Selous publish his 1927 book *Realities of Bird Life*.

Perhaps Selous's most prescient observation was that 'the habits of animals are really as scientific as their anatomies, and as professors of them, when once made, would be as good as their brothers.' He believed in the creative power of natural and sexual selection to shape purposive, intelligent actions, and, as Huxley noted, was 'alert...to the small divergences in behaviour whereby a species may become altered or split in two'. In his last book, *Evolution of the Habits of Birds* (1933), Selous drew on his extensive body of knowledge to describe bird behaviour in evolutionary terms. Huxley pursued this goal further. In a 1916 paper marrying ornithology to biology, Huxley outlined the ways and means of approaching animal behaviour, as an evolutionist, a physiologist and psychologist. He later befriended two young zoologists, Konrad Lorenz and Niko Tinbergen, who went farther still, uniting several lines of inquiry to form a new science of the 'habits of animals' and their 'anatomies' such as Selous envisaged, namely ethology.

'I am as much of a hermit as I am mercifully allowed to be,' Selous once wrote, suggesting his wife's tolerance of his absences and his dislike of social outings and family affairs. In the 1920s, when their children had families of their own, Fanny and Edmund moved to Wyke Castle, a mid-nineteenth-century confection with an outsized drum tower in Dorset. In 1923 Fanny founded a local branch of the Woman's Institute there, an organisation established during the First World War to encourage women's role in food production. It may be assumed that Fanny never wore a bird hat to her meetings and frowned on those who did, and that she understood the pride and pleasure her husband took in the work that defined him. Writing was an important part of it, a faculty Selous honed to communicate the marvels he beheld, like synchronous flocking, or murmuration:

And now, more and faster than the eye can take it in, band grows upon band, the air is heavy with the ceaseless sweep of pinions, till, glinting and gleaming, their weary wayfaring turned to swiftest arrows of triumphant flight – toil become ecstasy, prose [become] an epic song – with rush and roar of wings, with a mighty commotion, all sweep, together, into one enormous cloud. And still they circle; now dense like a polished roof, now disseminated like the meshes of

some vast all-heaven-sweeping net, now darkening, now flashing out
a million rays of light, wheeling, rending, tearing, darting, crossing,
and piercing one another: a madness in the sky.

Summing up the 'shaping and driving forces' of his life, Edmund wrote:
'Joy in all wild life and its surroundings, with another joy in Darwin and
a social-shunning disposition and an intellectual love of truth, too.'

In later years, to assist his brother's biographer J. G. Millais, Edmund
wrote briefly, if reflectively, about the shaping and driving forces of Fred's
life. He must have read at least the first of Fred's eight books, *A Hunter's
Wanderings in Africa* (1881), about tracking elephant, which is harder than
you'd think. 'In the thick bush, an elephant, though so large an animal, is
a thing easily lost sight of,' Fred wrote. On one occasion, Fred spotted an
elephant that had spotted him first and stood on guard, with 'ears
extended, his trunk stretched straight out, and his wicked, vicious-looking
eyes gazing in our direction, [standing] ready to charge'. Fred shot him in
the chest; the elephant dropped to its knees, then rose and walked away.
Meanwhile four other elephants advanced in single file, and figuring the
one he'd lately been 'paying attention to, was all but done for', Fred shot
the last of the newcomers in the shoulder. That didn't kill him, so Fred
followed and reloaded, calling out, 'Hi there! Woho, old man!' When the
elephant turned, whether from 'fatal curiosity, or perhaps a wish for
vengeance', Fred 'planted a four-ounce ball in his chest'. The elephant
staggered a few paces, gave 'a fierce shake of the head, and slowly sinking
down, surrendered his tough old spirit'.

One can imagine Edmund shaking his head over his brother's prose,
so spare, so soaked in blood. Fred killed 31 lions and 106 elephants in
addition to other animals, including buffalo, hippo and countless ante-
lope, a relatively modest 'career bag' compared to the 700-1,000 elephants
previous hunters claimed to have slayed. Fred nonetheless enjoyed the
title of naturalist for his writing about African wildlife and the specimens
of flora and fauna he contributed to the British Museum of Natural
History. This must have irked Edmund, who had a higher sense of purpose, whereas Fred was preoccupied with notoriety and the belief that
wealth was a measure of success. Yet both brothers revelled in nature.

The ruler of the Ndebele nation, Lobengula, granted Fred permission
to hunt in his kingdom, which comprised most of present-day Zimbabwe.
Fred enjoyed proving his courage and stamina to older, more

experienced hunters, as he penetrated the interior accompanied by savvy locals. He witnessed the festival of Inxwala, when Lobengula's 25,000 warriors assembled in full regalia, with spears and oxhide shields, chanting and dancing through the night, 'as imposing a spectacle as any race of savages in the world'. 'Savage' was commonly and unselfconsciously used by Fred and his English contemporaries, who saw themselves as an enlightened, civilising force in an otherwise dark continent, a race apart. Fred lacked the breadth and flexibility to meet Africans on common ground, since the very ground was adversarial; he came to it armed and licensed to kill.

He must have nonetheless envied the locals' knowledge of their surroundings, which was to them as second nature. Perhaps that's why Fred's relationship with an African woman lasted years; she was the closest he could get. It was customary for hunters deprived of white women's company to openly partner with local women. The unnamed woman who lived with Fred bore him two sons, lost to history. He abandoned them during a dark night of the soul, when someone short-changed him in a half-baked business deal, which happened more than once. When hunting proved less profitable than he'd hoped, he got involved in schemes for mining concessions, negotiating with tribal leaders whose favour he later exploited to assist his friend, Cecil Rhodes, in commandeering their land.

Whatever his qualities, Frederick Selous was an imperialist in tooth and claw, a righteous dominator. He wanted to hunt and adventure, and if expanding the British Empire was part of the deal, he was all in. People spoke of his modesty, though reticence is perhaps the better word. At some point he'd turned inward, grown wary of what lurks in the bush and in the unknowable minds of men. People disappointed him. The Ndebele were of great interest initially but he grew to despise their ruthlessness; the Mashona he found more appropriately docile until they rebelled to stop the occupation of their lands. He married late, in England, at 43. His wife, Gladys Maddy, was 20, raised in a rural vicarage, and taken with him. They had a home in Surrey but moved to Africa in 1895, when Lobengula's former kingdom was named Rhodesia. They had three sons; one lived less than a week, and another died at 20 fighting for Britain during the First World War. And so did Fred, at 64, as captain of the Royal Fusiliers' 25th Battalion during an East Africa Campaign skirmish between British and German colonialists. He was doing reconnaissance on the banks of the Rufiji River in Tanzania when he stood, raised his binoculars and took a bullet in the head.

Edmund saw his brother's fate as preordained, a residual curse of their maternal line, 'the [Bruce] patronymic, which, from one war to another, has borne the malevolent influence. None have come back, either wounded, invalided or at all. All killed outright.' The upside of his ancestry was that it facilitated Fred's lucky escape from the 'settled professions' he loathed. Edmund felt Fred would agree that his chosen career 'put the particular circumstances of that event of his life, in which, of all others, he would esteem himself most happy and fortunate – I mean his death – upon a footing of certainty'. Aside from implying that Fred lived and died by the gun, Edmund felt his brother would have been proud to fall fighting for King and Country, a clean shot, no pitiful staggering, no sickness or fraught goodbyes, only biographies and statues in due time.

Edmund lived to the age of 77, '[a] tragic figure in his old age, with his passion for the lovely wild things of the earth that are being relentlessly driven to their doom by cruel and indifferent [industrial] man', wrote American ornithologist Margaret Morse Nice, in her tribute to Selous, one of two that appeared in specialist journals following his death. His accomplishments were lately revisited in Richard Burckhardt's *Patterns of Behavior*, from 2005, a masterfully contextualised history of the science of ethology that illumines the remarkable lives of those who shaped the discipline. Research continues to add to Selous's understanding of bird behaviour. Data obtained in recent well-funded, large-scope studies would have excited him, such as that compiled by biologist and comparative psychologist Louis Lefebvre, who agreed with Selous's 'boots on the ground' approach and invented a system for assessing bird cognition, based on their ability to use tools and solve problems. Studies of bird societies would have likewise intrigued him, affirming his observation that personalities differ within groups, but additionally showing that the more daring individuals will set out together to scout territory and network with communities of the same and different species.

Interest in birds is nowadays soaring. In 2020, Cornell University's Lab of Ornithology reported above-average numbers of citizen-submitted sightings to eBird, their database documenting bird activity worldwide. In the US, the sale of bird feeders is way up, with $2.2 billion projected for 2021, and 'avitourism', travel to observe birds in their native habitat, is a growing industry. In the UK, over a million people participated in 2021 in the world's largest communal wildlife survey, the Big Garden Birdwatch, organised by theRoyal Society for the Protection of Birds. They counted 17 million birds, while noting that they've grown scarcer; an estimated 40 million fewer fill the UK skies now than 50 years ago. The cumulative effects of pesticides and fertiliser in the seeds and plants birds forage, in addition to climate change, pollution and urbanisation, are all taking their toll. In short, more people than ever are watching birds disappear.

To study birds is to contemplate flight, 'the dream and joy of glorious motion', wrote Edmund Selous, 'cradled in the air, looking like a shadow upon it'. It's one of the ways birds outdo us, and the reason civilisations past saw in them the divine. 'Joy' and 'wonder' crop up repeatedly in Selous's writing, hinting at the most mysterious bird behaviour of all: their timeless, effortless ability to elicit uplifting emotion in humans. It's as if they were asking, in an off-wing kind of way, for us to not only watch but to join them in belonging to nature by simply acknowledging that like them, for better or worse, we already do.

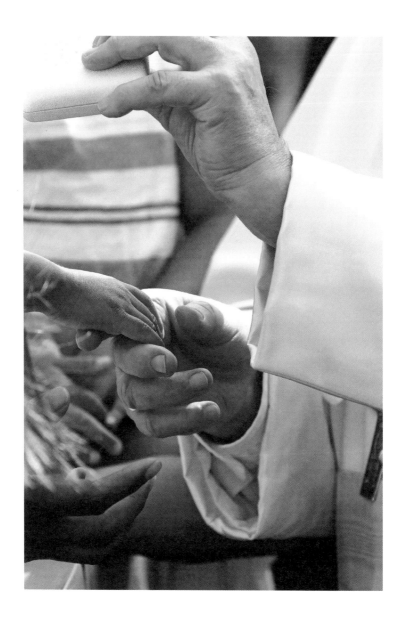

Pope Francis greeting visitors at a
general audience, 2021.

HUMANISM MATTERS IN THE AGE OF AI

Nick Spencer

Of all the things Pope Francis might have been expected to mention in *Fratelli Tutti: On Fraternity and Social Friendship*, his most recent encyclical letter, humanism was probably not one of them.

Encyclical letters are the heavy artillery of papal communications, reaching further than the multitude of other letters, speeches and messages that emanate from the Vatican. In this one, the leader of the world's one billion or so Catholics wrote about the damage done by 'illusory' communication; about the destruction of human dignity in the treatment of refugees; and about the toxicity of a wasteful culture. Among this, in paragraph 86, at the end of a long chapter about the Good Samaritan, he slipped in a mention of 'humanism'.

This was not an antagonistic reference, despite the association of humanism with secularism and hostility to organised religion. Indeed, the Pope was more critical of (some) religious people than he was of the irreligious: 'Those who claim to be unbelievers can sometimes put God's will into practice better than believers.' Pope Francis seemed to find in humanism precisely what we need to resist the kinds of violent nationalism, xenophobia and contempt for difference that plague the world today.

His former Anglican counterpart in the UK, Rowan Williams, makes a similar point in his book, *Looking East in Winter*. Drawing on centuries of Eastern Orthodox spiritual reflection, the book turns on the idea of 'liturgical humanism'. The former Archbishop of Canterbury laments the 'the loss of an authentic humanism' in our time, and seeks instead 'the [kind of] "humanism" in which [there is] a vision of every human face as the focus of self-forgetting love'. It is in embracing this 'integral humanism' – a phrase we will return to – that humanity can face the 'notably wintry world' of today.

That such prominent Christian figures speak warmly of a movement that is, in the popular mind at least, basically anti-religious, may seem odd. Why are the Pope and the former Archbishop of Canterbury writing so positively about humanism?

The answer lies in its history, which is more complex and interesting than its current formulation suggests. The political philosopher John Gray wrote a book about liberalism having two faces. Humanism is much the same: it has a religious face and an anti-religious one, but the former predates the latter by a long time.

If people are in any way familiar with the idea of religious – specifically Christian – humanism, it will be through eminent Renaissance men of letters, most famously Desiderius Erasmus. The late medieval discipline of *studia humanitatis* was the study of texts from the ancient world, primarily for their grammatical and rhetorical qualities, and the scholars who practised it were called *umanista*. Although they often delicately negotiated the different worlds of classical Rome and medieval Christendom, there was little sense that the two were irreconcilable. Indeed, in the words of church historian Diarmaid MacCulloch, 'the vast majority of humanists were patently sincere Christians who wished to apply their enthusiasm to the exploration and proclamation of their faith.' This applied not only to Catholics like Erasmus but to Protestants, including John Calvin, whose first published work was a commentary on Seneca the Younger's *De Clementia*. Writing and thinking well – humanely – was prized across the theological spectrum.

In time, the term 'humanist' drifted away from someone who was essentially a grammarian or rhetorician to meaning someone who studied human nature and human affairs. Thus, when the first publication to be titled *The Humanist* was published in 1757, the editor, an Irish clergyman, wrote that 'the title…implies neither more nor less, than that it interests itself in all the concerns of human nature,' and claimed the magazine was 'calculated to convey some little useful and entertaining knowledge of various kinds, historical, classical, natural, moral, and now-and-then a little religion into the readers' minds'.

By the later nineteenth century, the Renaissance had come to be identified as a distinct historical period allegedly characterised by a new approach to human dignity and a clean intellectual break with the Middle Ages. In reality, historians have shown there was far more continuity between the two periods than originally thought. Human dignity was not invented in fifteenth-century Florence. Nevertheless, the image of Renaissance *umanista* uncovering such dignity for the first time has persisted, and their original interest in style and rhetoric has faded from view. 'Humanism' became more about human dignity than prose style. Even after this shift, however, there was no sense that humanism was incompatible with Christianity.

Protestants – or at least some of them – had a harder job reconciling the humanistic commitment to dignity with their own theological understanding of human nature, which could be unremittingly bleak. Saved by faith alone, humans were wretched and helpless creatures, their good deeds little better than 'filthy rags', some argued. Such an uncompromising understanding of human nature faded over time, however, and the early years of the twentieth century saw Protestant publications such as the *Humanism and the Bible* series.

It was in the Catholic Church, however, that humanism was developed with the greatest commitment and sophistication. The single most important humanist work of the twentieth century came from Catholic Thomist philosopher Jacques Maritain in 1936. It was titled *Humanisme intégral* – hence Rowan Williams's phrase above. Translated into English two years later, the book argued that the dominant ideologies of the day – liberalism on one side and socialism and communism on the other – were in danger of flattening or crushing the complex, multifaceted 'human'. They risked turning people either into atomistic individuals or abolishing their uniqueness altogether in, and for the sake of, the collective good. In their place, Maritain argued, humanism needed to maintain both human uniqueness and dignity and our indissoluble connection to the wider public good. Humans were, he recognised, 'individuals', characterised by their differences from other humans, but also 'persons', beings formed by the bonds of love with others.

Along with philosophers such as Étienne Gilson, Maritain's work was to prove enormously influential. His ideas informed those of his friend Pope Pius XII, whose rhetoric around human dignity and rights in the 1940s helped change the intellectual climate, making it more amenable to the idea of legally recognised, generic 'human' rights. Maritain's ideas also helped form the basis of personalism, a movement grounded on a fundamental commitment to the dignity of the human person. Personalism would, in turn, prove hugely influential, shaping the tradition of post-war Christian Democracy in Germany, Netherlands, Spain and elsewhere; shaping the founding principles of the European Economic Community through the auspices of politicians such as Alcide De

Gasperi, Konrad Adenauer, Robert Schuman and Jean Monnet; and finally, in the drafting of the UN Declaration of Human Rights, which mentions the individual only once but the '[human] person' five times and 'personality' three times.

The tradition went on to influence post-war Catholic thought with one Pope after another praising humanism. Pope Paul VI talked about 'the principles of a true humanism'. John Paul II wrote about 'authentic humanism'. Pope Francis spoke of 'a genuine and profound humanism' and now, most recently, of the humanism inspired by faith. In this way, humanism has shown itself to be a thoroughly religious, and specifically Catholic, idea with a long history and wide reach.

So much for the first face. Humanism is also an anti-religious movement, and this constitutes its second face.

If you went looking for an atheist in the nineteenth century you would most likely find them under the label of freethinker, infidel, rationalist, sceptic, secularist or unbeliever. Few, if any, called themselves humanists. Nevertheless, as early as 1812, Samuel Taylor Coleridge could write of he 'who has passed from orthodoxy to the loosest Arminianism, and thence to Arianism, and thence to direct humanism [before falling] off into the hopeless abyss of atheism'. Coleridge's humanism was not so much anti-religious as deistic or Unitarian – someone who believed in God but without any doctrinal trappings, as his publisher Joseph Cottle suggested in 1837. In this regard, the commitment to the 'human' within humanism was always at least latently non-religious: easily hijacked to mean a commitment to the human as opposed to the divine.

This was precisely how it came to be deployed by the French philosopher Auguste Comte, grandfather of sociology, in the early nineteenth century, as he attempted to put the study of the human on a scientific footing. He set up a religion of humanity, which treated mankind, rather than God, as the object of worship. Comte's religion borrowed heavily from Catholicism but liberated itself from its more incredible theological and metaphysical claims. Even adapted, it did not flourish, especially in Britain, where its elaborate rituals put off a still predominantly Protestant population. The biologist Thomas Huxley once witheringly called it 'Catholicism minus Christianity'. It did, however, mutate by the end of the century into a gentler form of 'ethical humanism', which emerged in the ethical movement of the late Victorian period.

This comprised a series of societies for people who had lost their (usually Anglican) faith but who wanted to preserve the moral, ritual and community dimensions of their abandoned religion. The object of faith now, after Comte, was 'man', not God. Thus, when *The Humanist* – not the eighteenth-century journal of that name but a new organ of the ethical movement published in the 1920s – launched its opening edition, its front-page editorial was on 'The Religion of Humanism' which, it declared, was based on 'faith in man'.

In this way, the word was finally weaponised against its religious associations. F. J. Gould, a co-founder of the Rationalist Press Association, which *was* anti-religious, wrote in 1900 that humanism was 'a new idea [that] is actually displacing Theism…[and which] lies in contrast with Theism'. Humanism became a commitment to the human as opposed to the divine.

For a time, the two faces coexisted in relative harmony. When, in 1944, the BBC broadcast three talks about humanism, it engaged with scientific humanism with Julian Huxley, classical humanism with Gilbert Murray and Christian Humanism with J. H. Oldham. The three did not agree on everything – Oldham, for example, insisted that humanism needed theism – but there was little sense that, awkward bedfellows though they might be, divorce was imminent.

In the post-war period, however, Protestant (as opposed to Catholic) Christians often preferred to see only the non-religious dimension in humanism, and non-religious humanists increasingly stressed their antipathy to religion and, in some cases, steered humanism in a consciously anti-religious direction.

One recent history of post-war humanism shows that in some historically Protestant countries, non-religious humanism was primarily interested in questions of freedom of thought and expression. In these places – such as Britain, where nonconformists had long since done the heavy anticlerical lifting, and America, where the First Amendment prevented the confessionalisation of the state – humanism didn't need to be weaponised against religion. In other countries, however, particularly historically Catholic ones, the movement became a battering ram against the still-powerful clerical establishment, and humanist associations and unions founded in the 1950s and 60s campaigned on an anti-Catholic ticket, focusing on moral issues around abortion, marriage, divorce and the like.

This is a helpful categorisation, although it only goes so far. In the UK, for example, Catholicism was much less of a cultural force and the established churches were often in lockstep over cultural liberalisation. Yet that has not stopped anti-religious humanism from growing into a powerful movement. This has much to do with some supremely articulate anti-religious humanist campaigners, but the rise of anti-religious humanism in the UK is still a subject that requires academic attention. After all, it is a long time since England or Scotland has had the equivalent of ultramontane Catholicism or American-style religious fundamentalism looming over its public debates. The Troubles of Northern Ireland can only explain so much.

However complex its history, non-religious humanism is now a powerful force in our intellectual landscape, all but eclipsing the longer and richer tradition of Christian humanism. Moreover, unveiling the two faces of humanism helps us navigate the current situation, when for the first time in living memory there are genuinely anti-humanist threats on the horizon.

What you consider to be anti-humanist does, of course, depend on what you consider to be humanist. But if you judge humanism to involve a commitment to human dignity, rights, rationality, morality and freedom – a list of attributes on which most religious and non-religious humanists would agree – it is not so far-fetched to see how they might be in danger.

In the immediate term, a number of these beliefs will be stress-tested by the rise of populist movements and of authoritarian regimes around the world, whose commitment to a humanistic understanding of the person is dubious at best. However, such threats pale into insignificance when placed alongside the potential danger to humans posed by genetic engineering and AI.

Kazuo Ishiguro's brilliant novel *Klara and the Sun* captures, with characteristic subtlety and narrative intelligence, a world in which humans have been formed and deformed, lifted and left behind by advanced genetic engineering and new AI technology. In a similar way, Martin Rees, Astronomer Royal, recently remarked to me in an interview for *Reading our Times*, my books and ideas podcast, 'We've got no guarantee that the [artificial] entities who are our progeny a few hundred years from now will have anything more than an algorithmic understanding of our emotions and how we behaved.' Novelists and others have been warning for years about the prospect of a 'Posthuman Future', to quote a Francis Fukuyama title. Their predictions may now have some substance.

You do not need to be alarmist about a fully post-human future to imagine that our long-standing commitment to the human may be under threat. And it is for this reason that we would benefit from healing the schism in humanism. There are differences between the two faces, as there are within any party, such as in politics. But more important is the shared commitment to the human, which will become vital in the twenty-first century as we are faced with opportunities to edit or remake humanity altogether.

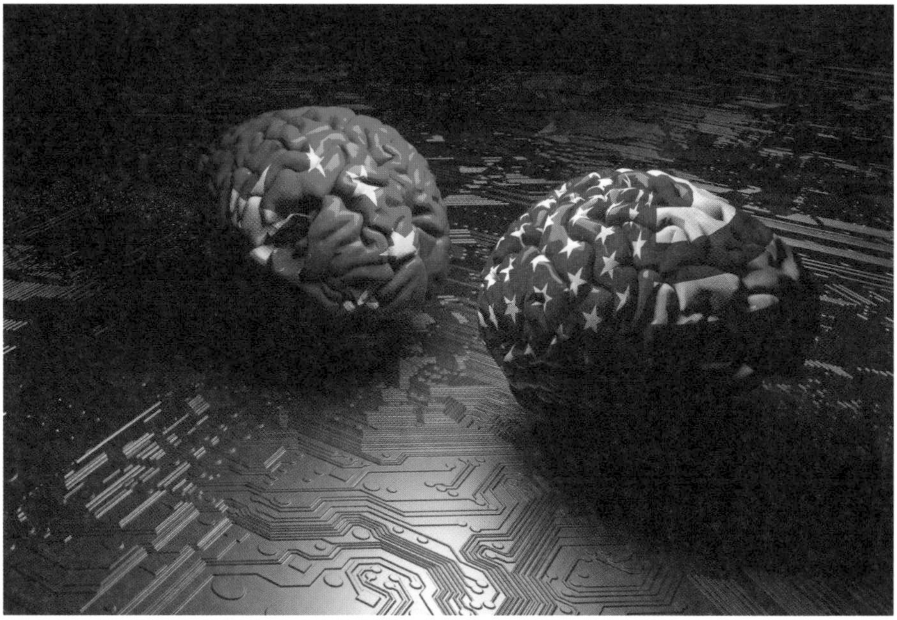

China and the USA compete about technology.

THE ENDLESS FRONTIER

Sharon Weinberger

On 21 April 2021, in a rare moment of unity in Washington DC, the White House endorsed a bipartisan bill known as the Endless Frontier Act that would commit $100 billion in funding over the next five years into research intended to help maintain US technological leadership over China.

In a country that over the last three years has seen two impeachment trials of a president, an attempt to overturn the results of a presidential election, and a violent riot at the Capitol, this support from both Democrats and Republicans is no small feat. We live in a time, after all, where politicians on the left and right can't seem to agree on the causes or dangers of climate change (around which there is a clear scientific consensus), or whether face masks can help slow the spread of Covid-19 (they indeed can, according to the peer-reviewed scientific literature), yet concerns about being overtaken by China in science and technology have brought the two political parties together, even if briefly.

The Endless Frontier Act, named after the influential report written in 1945 for President Franklin D. Roosevelt, would put that $100bn into a new directorate in the National Science Foundation modelled after the storied Defense Advanced Research Projects Agency, the Pentagon department credited with developing the internet, driverless cars and drones. The new directorate, according to the proposed legislation, would be focused on key technologies, ranging from artificial intelligence to synthetic biology – all areas where China has excelled in recent years.

The Endless Frontier Act comes amid a global pandemic that at April 2021 had already claimed three million lives, while spurring some of the most accelerated scientific progress in recent memory by way of new vaccines to combat the virus. Particularly in the United States, Operation Warp Speed, the government programme that supported several vaccine candidates now being injected into people's arms every day, will likely go down in history as an example of extraordinarily successful state-assisted innovation.

The Endless Frontier Act harkens back to an earlier era of ambitious government expansion into the sciences. After the Second World War, the government became the largest supporter of science in the United States, giving it the ability to create entirely new fields of research, such as computer science, and heavily influence the direction of existing fields, such as physics.

Today, however, in many areas of research, whether artificial intelligence or biotechnology, government spending is often overshadowed by private sector funding, whether through venture capital or other forms of investment. Even space exploration, once the exclusive domain of government, is facing competition from private industry.

More than 75 years after the original 'Endless Frontier' report, the landscape of government-supported science and technology has shifted drastically, particularly in the United States, and governments have given little thought to how to adapt their approach. Today, not only has the US government largely backed away from some of its most ambitious post-war ideas for sponsoring basic science, but it has also increasingly latched onto a model of innovation – such as the idea of high-risk 'moonshots' – that fundamentally misunderstands the history of government-sponsored innovation and what is required to achieve significant breakthroughs. Some government-sponsored programmes, like Operation Warp Speed, will still be successful, but it's likely that many others without clearly defined goals will fail. Understanding what works and why could be the key to avoiding some of the costliest failures.

The origins of 'The Endless Frontier' report date to 17 November 1944, when President Roosevelt wrote to Vannevar Bush, the head of the wartime Office of Scientific Research and Development, asking how the country could take advantage of the military innovations being developed so they could be 'profitably employed in times of peace'.

The president's vision was broad – focused on the betterment of the country and its people, not necessarily on national security or staying ahead of other countries. He wrote:

The information, the techniques, and the research experience developed by the Office of Scientific Research and Development and by the thousands of scientists in the universities and in private industry, should be used in the days of peace ahead for the improvement of the national health, the creation of new enterprises bringing new jobs, and the betterment of the national standard of living.

In July 1945, just weeks before the United States dropped atomic bombs (the most significant and secret of those wartime technologies) on Nagasaki and Hiroshima, Bush delivered his final report to the president. In it, he spelled out a vision that encompassed everything from health to employment. 'Progress in the war against disease depends upon a flow of new scientific knowledge. New products, new industries, and more jobs require continuous additions to knowledge of the laws of nature, and the application of that knowledge to practical purposes,' he wrote. 'Similarly, our defense against aggression demands new knowledge so that we can develop new and improved weapons. This essential, new knowledge can be obtained only through basic scientific research.'

Bush's report laid out a bold plan for the federal government to take a leading role in funding basic research. Scientists would lead this effort, rather than bureaucrats or politicians, ensuring the focus on the expansion of knowledge rather than short-term policy imperatives. Even if its most ambitious recommendations were never fulfilled, Bush's vision of government patronage for the sciences set the stage for much of the postwar order. 'The Endless Frontier' led to a fundamental rethinking of the relationship between the government, science and technological innovation. 'For science to serve as a powerful factor in our national welfare, applied research both in Government and in industry must be vigorous,' Bush wrote.

Following Bush's advice, the National Science Foundation was established in 1950, signalling the government's permanent role in furthering research. Less than a decade later, however, another event would have a profound impact on science policy. In October 1957, the Soviet Union launched Sputnik, the world's first artificial satellite, beating the United States to space. While Sputnik was not a complete shock to the scientific community, which had been watching Soviet progress in rockets, the launch created a political opportunity for critics of President Dwight D. Eisenhower. It also highlighted some of the shortcomings in the US government's approach to space technology, which lacked a central authority.

A few months later, President Eisenhower authorised the creation of the Advanced Research Projects Agency (it later became known as

DARPA, when 'defense' was added to its title), which would consolidate and accelerate the nation's rocket programmes. The agency was also given a broad remit 'to direct such research and development projects being performed within the Department of Defense as the Secretary of Defense may designate'. In other words, the agency could work in any area of science that the Pentagon's leadership wanted, cutting through red tape to quickly start research and advance new technologies. And that's precisely what it did in a surprisingly broad range of fields.

Within a few years of being founded, DARPA began funding computer science at universities and labs across the country, helping to lay the foundations for an entirely new field of research. Within a decade this research led to a nascent proposal for a computer network known as the ARPANET, the predecessor to the modern internet.

Over the next few decades, DARPA managed to churn out a series of notable innovations, some useful primarily to the military, such as stealth aircraft, but others, including voice recognition, driverless cars and unmanned aircraft, with broad commercial applications. Its pursuit of high-risk, high-payoff research became a model that, by the 2000s, the government tried to replicate elsewhere, including in the Energy Department, Homeland Security and the Office of National Intelligence. In most cases, those new agencies stumbled.

Even so, the attempts to replicate the DARPA model continue. Most recently, President Biden on 29 April suggested to a joint session of Congress a new DARPA for health. 'The National Institutes of Health, the NIH, I believe, should create a similar advanced research projects agency for health,' he said. 'And that would – here's what it would do: it would have a singular purpose, to develop breakthroughs to prevent, detect and treat diseases like Alzheimer's, diabetes and cancer.'

More than a decade ago, amid several of the already faltering attempts, I asked one of DARPA's former directors, Stephen Lukasik, if there was any appropriate field for creating a DARPA-like agency. He mused that one obvious possibility would be an agency to address climate change. Scientifically, it would be the right problem to look at, but, he cautioned, there were already too many entrenched interests in place, such as the fossil fuel industry.

The problem is not just scientific, but economic and political, and those are factors that a science agency is ill-equipped to address. 'In the case of space we had a national problem with no existing structure,' he said, explaining DARPA's initial success. 'As soon as you say, "What about energy? Healthcare? Homeland security?" you have a huge structure.'

The best example, he suggested half facetiously, would be an agency dedicated to protecting the earth from being struck by an asteroid. 'We could pull off a DARPA for that, because there isn't an anti-asteroid infrastructure in place,' he said. 'In general, the threat would be universally understood, the impact would be universally disastrous, and it would be scientifically challenging.'

Imagining a mad scramble of government-funded scientists working on technologies to divert an asteroid impact may sound far-fetched (in part because it is the plot device for several Hollywood films), but so too was the idea of a global pandemic prior to 2020.

When the first cases of Covid-19, the disease caused by the novel coronavirus, were identified in the United States in January 2020, the government was unprepared on almost every level. The National Strategic Stockpile, which included N-95 respirators, didn't have anywhere near the inventories needed to deal with a pandemic, despite years of warnings from scientists that one was coming. There were scientific stumbles as well, demonstrated by the initially botched attempt by the Centers for Disease Control and Prevention to develop its own Covid-19 test. In another sign of the ill-prepared times, when the pandemic hit the United States, the US Army Medical Research Institute of Infectious Diseases at Fort Detrick, the military lab responsible for defending against biological threats, was closed due to safety violations.

Amazingly, amid an otherwise chaotic response to the pandemic, the Trump administration initiated Operation Warp Speed, a $10 billion programme to accelerate development and production of vaccines for Covid-19. Even as the United States lagged behind in medical supplies, testing and other efforts to contain the spread of the virus, the public–private partnership was by any measure a stunning success, leading to several vaccine candidates approved by the Food and Drug Administration in under a year. As a result, the United States, which had one of the worst track records for controlling the spread of Covid-19, quickly became one of the top countries for progress on vaccinations.

That leads to a critical question: why did Operation Warp Speed succeed, and what lessons does that offer for future government-sponsored programmes? One of the key aspects of the operation, similar to other successful government-sponsored research efforts at DARPA, was that it had a clear customer. The government wasn't just sponsoring the research, it was also the customer for the product, ultimately buying hundreds of millions of doses of the vaccines from the participating companies while also smoothing the path for vaccine approval through a fast-track mechanism known as emergency use authorisation.

By contrast, progress with vaccinations in Europe has been rocky, in part because there is no central acquisition authority. While the United States has faced hiccups in the distribution and administration of the vaccine, which is largely handled by the state and local authorities, the federal government's purchase of the vaccines helped accelerate overall progress.

The pandemic has demonstrated that the federal government still can bring resources to bear to help solve an urgent scientific problem rapidly. Without Operation Warp Speed, pharmaceutical companies would still have moved forward, but it's doubtful that Moderna, which had never previously brought a drug to market, would have produced a vaccine in under a year without the nearly half a billion dollar federal government investment the company received. And while Pfizer didn't take federal money for development of its vaccine, it did benefit from an advance purchase order under Operation Warp Speed, without which it likely wouldn't have moved as quickly as it did. Having a guaranteed market for an innovation, thanks to a government purchase, can be as valuable as research dollars.

In fact, one thing that Operation Warp Speed should teach us is that the ability of the government to direct and accelerate innovation depends in large part on its ability to guarantee a readily available market for technologies. In the case of the Covid-19 vaccine, the government's investment in development was important, but the guarantee of a large market – i.e. the entire American population – was even more critical.

The success of Operation Warp Speed thus raises a critical question for the Endless Frontier Act. Even if the government funnels $100bn into new research, who will be the customer for the resulting technologies? Possibly the military, or the private sector, but there's no guarantee they will be interested or have a specific need for the innovations that come out of this research. Any government research manager can talk for hours about the 'valley of death' for innovations that emerge from academia and labs only to die on the vine.

Providing more funding for science and technology, as the Endless Frontier Act proposes to do, is laudable and will have some benefits for the country, but the question is whether the government has the political will and patience for the type of long-term commitment that requires. And without a clear customer for the scientific and technological innovations this new directorate would fund, it's unlikely to produce the type of breakthroughs that lawmakers typically expect to maintain steady funding over many years.

Perhaps most fundamentally, the idea of making this directorate a 'new DARPA' should not inspire confidence in the results, given the series of mostly forgettable 'DARPAs' for energy and homeland security. One reason for those lacklustre results is that the new agencies have never enjoyed the independence or funding that the original DARPA enjoyed. More fundamental, however, is that those attempts to replicate DARPA never had a clear customer, like the Pentagon, with its now more than $700bn annual budget and central acquisition authority. Who was going to buy the innovations produced by the energy ARPA? Certainly not the Department of Energy. Private industry possibly, but only if those innovations are immediately profitable, which is usually not the case. Similarly, the Department of Homeland Security, which is made up of myriad agencies, has no central authority for purchasing technology.

If the goal of the new Endless Frontier legislation were simply to reinvigorate the country's science base, that would be laudable and perhaps sensible. But the gulf between 'The Endless Frontier' report of 1945 and the Endless Frontier Act of 2021 is the gulf between Vannevar Bush's vision of broad-based scientific support that would advance the nation's welfare, and a bill inspired mainly by competition with China. To bridge that gap will require political leadership that can reimagine a relationship between the state and science that fits the realities of the twenty-first century.

At work on the Enigma machine, 1943.

THE ART AND SCIENCE OF
INTELLIGENCE IN WAR

Hew Strachan

When I was growing up in Edinburgh in the 1950s, my father would depart for his office clutching a battered, brown leather briefcase. The briefcase, he told my brother and me, had accompanied him on a Commando raid in the Second World War.

In September 1939 my father was reading modern languages at Cambridge. He had spent part of 1938 in Berlin and his German was fluent and colloquial. Called up by the Army, he went to the Military Equitation School in January 1940 to train for a small mounted unit intended to collect intelligence behind enemy lines – presumably a sort of Long Range Desert Group on horses rather than in trucks. During the Battle of Britain, he exchanged his horse for a motorbike and travelled between prisoner-of-war camps, interrogating shot-down German aircrew. In February 1941 he was sent overseas for the first time, as an intelligence officer on a raid to destroy the cod liver oil factories on the Lofoten Islands, off the coast of Norway. Those on the raid were told that the fish oil was for making bombs, not for consumption by growing babies. Lord Lovat, the Commando leader, came along for the ride and, according to my father, brought his stalking rifle; my father had his briefcase.

Shortly before he died in 2000, I asked my father what the purpose of the raid had been. He repeated the same story: to destroy the factories, a mission that had been successfully accomplished without loss of life. I told him he was wrong. The British had captured an Enigma machine, whose settings were changed every day in order to encrypt German signals, and – even more importantly – its enciphering tables. The coup had enabled Bletchley Park to begin to read German naval traffic. My father was not given to blasphemy, but his face expressed astonishment. I was amazed for a different reason. His credulity had trumped his rationality. He was an intelligence officer and in 1943 he would go on to work in MI (Plans) in North Africa, processing German signal intercepts into actionable information. In order not to reveal their sources, the British could not immediately attack Axis convoys sailing across the Mediterranean but had to give the enemy good grounds for attributing their responses to more obvious methods of detection, frequently aerial reconnaissance. This much my father had divulged to me in 1974, the year in which Frederick Winterbotham, a wartime MI6 officer, had revealed the prime source of allied intelligence for the first time in *The Ultra Secret*, so breaching a confidence which many, my father included, had kept for 30 years.

While the Commandos destroyed the fish factories, rounded up quislings and looted useful equipment, my father – or so I fancy – went to the telegraph office and put everything he could find into his briefcase. He gave me a copy of Heinz Guderian's pamphlet, *Die Panzertruppen und ihr Zusammenwirken mit den anderen Waffen* (Mechanised forces in employment with other arms), which he acquired in this sweep and which either he had opted not to hand over on his return or his masters had concluded was now out of date (it was published in 1937). He may even have seized a codebook and so helped fulfil the raid's objective but, if he had, he remained unaware of it. His gullibility was crucial to the operation – if he had been captured and interrogated, he would not have been able to reveal information he did not possess.

My father's Lofoten briefcase lies at the intersection of the impact of new technologies and their role in wartime intelligence with older and more human methods of deception and influence. When Carl von Clausewitz wrote *On War* in the aftermath of the Napoleonic Wars, he was sceptical of intelligence's value. Much of it rested on rumour which could not be tested and was liable to exaggeration. It was also probably out of date. The information which had proved so useful to Napoleon himself was topographical. Accurate mapping enabled him to plan his lines of march, to anticipate the possible loss of time created by obstacles such as rivers and forests, and to find viable routes so that his armies could threaten alternative objectives. But in many contexts, not least those of nineteenth-century colonial warfare, armies were like explorers, surveying as they went and collecting anthropological and ethnographic information, which would underpin the assumptions of empire. Technology played a key role in cartography, just as it did in the production of naval charts, but it only provided the broad contours of a campaign. The acquisition of tactical and time-sensitive intelligence was rudimentary. A cavalry patrol would struggle to penetrate far into enemy positions and was in danger of revealing its own commander's intentions as it did so. Finding the enemy was even harder at sea, where unpredictable and variable weather could enable fleets to hide as effectively as did the expanse of the oceans.

At the beginning of the twentieth century, wireless revolutionised the potential applications of intelligence in war. By transmitting directives through the ether, it conveyed a commander's intentions in a format which was publicly accessible, and did so in real time. To minimise these dangers, messages were relayed in code, but the processes of enciphering and decoding themselves took time and so undercut the gains in speed. In 1914, during the last week of the July crisis which led to the outbreak of the First World War, governments could sometimes intercept each other's diplomatic traffic but still struggled to do so fast enough to get inside each other's decision-making loop. A signal sent from an ambassador to his head of state at home had to be enciphered, transmitted and then decoded before it arrived on the statesman's desk. In a fast-changing situation, the statesman at home might be reacting to yesterday's events while his adversary might have learned his ambassador's views through intercepts at least as quickly as he did.

When the war broke out, tactical intelligence was frequently too time-sensitive to permit such delays. As armies manoeuvred across Europe in August 1914, speed could trump security in the transmission of information and intentions. Units, most notoriously within the Russian 2nd Army in its invasion of East Prussia, communicated with each other in clear speech, so providing the enemy with real-time intelligence that, in this case, contributed to the defeat at Tannenberg. But they did so in the hope that, even with this advantage, the enemy would be too late in his responses. Ciphers in any case did not provide full security; any wireless traffic indicated enemy activity, especially when it increased in quantity, and proximity as its volume intensified. The only perfect way to avoid detection was to observe radio silence but that, in turn, incurred penalties. At Jutland on 31 May 1916, David Beatty used flags to signal to his battle cruisers, with the result that orders were missed or misinterpreted in the smoke. The British Grand Fleet was given the chance to intercept the German High Seas Fleet because German ships chattered to each other with helpful volubility, but, once it was at sea, British naval intelligence were fearful of sending its commander, Jellicoe, raw intercepts and, as a result, he lost his moment to achieve a 'decisive' victory.

For much of both world wars, British naval intelligence was able to read German signals. By the end of 1914 the Royal Navy had secured three German code books. In 1915 SMS *Königsberg*, a German light cruiser blockaded by British ships in the Rufiji delta in East Africa, thought its signals were being read, but its warning was not taken seriously; this was despite the fact that in March 1916 a blockade runner which observed radio silence managed to deliver supplies to the German forces in East Africa when one that did not failed. The High Seas Fleet attributed its encounter with the Grand Fleet at Jutland to bad luck, not to poor wireless discipline.

In the Second World War, the British again struck lucky. The Poles had acquired an Enigma machine and they brought it to Britain. Enigma enabled both speed of transmission and secrecy. Although it was compromised from early in the war, it took time for the British to be able to read Enigma signals (using an early form of computer) and there were periods when the British were effectively locked out. Despite what would seem, in hindsight, to be mounting evidence, Germany's faith in the security of its signals remained as resilient in the Second World War as in the First. It put its trust in technology and, as a result, came to believe that evidence of information leaks had to be attributed to other factors. Human intelligence – spying – became one way of explaining the apparently inexplicable.

Spy stories and espionage myth-making flourished during and after the First World War. Although both sides used agents, their actual achievements were outstripped by the claims of post-war films and fiction. Mata Hari, the Dutch-born double agent executed by the French in 1917, embodied the allure of the female spy as *femme fatale*. This suited the intelligence services. Human intelligence was never likely to produce actionable information with the speed and in the quantity provided by signals intelligence, but that dependence could be covered by public self-deception and its appetite for fictional secret agents. The most successful British writer in this genre, John Buchan, was simultaneously running British propaganda. He almost certainly knew what technology was delivering through signals intelligence, but his novels highlighted only human intelligence.

Buchan's last First World War spy story, *Mr Standfast*, takes the German offensive of March 1918 as its denouement. It ends with a battle in the air – the second technological revolution during the First World War to transform intelligence, particularly at the tactical level. The movements of the German armies as they swung into France from Belgium in August 1914 were tracked by French aircraft and revealed the moment when the manoeuvre that culminated with the victory of the Marne could be put into effect. When photography was allied to aerial reconnaissance, armies could collect information from deep inside enemy lines and have time to analyse it. They could check their developing assumptions by sending out further flights, and they could correlate their findings with other sources of intelligence, including signals intercepts and night raids. To be sure, bad weather, short winter days, darkness, deception and camouflage could enable the enemy to evade aerial observation, as the Germans did at Verdun in January 1916 before attacking in February, and as they were to do again in the Ardennes in December 1944. But the general effect was to make a surprise attack much harder to achieve and so to reinforce deadlock, most evidently in the First World War but also in the Second. Manoeuvre was now predicated on first achieving aerial supremacy over the battlefield so that the enemy was denied the opportunity to realise what was afoot.

The abundance of information furnished by new technologies in twentieth-century wars presented a fresh challenge for human agency. The issue now was less the collection of intelligence and more its assessment. Individual intercepts conveyed information that was often trivial or routine when analysed in isolation, and only gained significance when read in a wider context. The major contribution which the breaking of Enigma made to the conduct of the war was the cumulative ability to read the German order of battle, to know when units were being moved and whither they were bound. Similarly, aerial observation required successive images of the same location in order to detect change – the construction of new positions, the siting of guns or the effect of bombing. The expertise and experience required for the interpretation of signals or photographs might result in the correct conclusions but not in the right decisions. Commanders could still not know exactly what was in the mind of the enemy; they might be looking at a deliberate deception, as the Germans did in June 1944. They were encouraged by wireless traffic and dummy tanks to believe that a large army under George S. Patton was being mustered in England for a second Allied landing in France at the Pas de Calais. Commanders could be given and accept perfectly accurate intelligence but still only possess a partial insight into enemy intentions, and so misread either the time or the direction of an enemy attack. And they could simply reject what they were told because it did not conform with what they wanted to hear. Bernard Montgomery, commanding the 21st Army Group as it advanced into the Low Countries in September 1944, refused to accept the Ultra intelligence which placed two Panzer divisions in the location of the Rhine bridge at Arnhem, which he planned to take with lightly equipped airborne forces. Montgomery failed.

Despite the contribution made by technology to intelligence collection, it neither prevents wishful thinking nor provides foolproof answers to war's conduct. In the recent conflicts in Iraq and Afghanistan, the United States and its allies have enjoyed massive advantages in signals intelligence but have suffered from a lack of human intelligence. In planning the aerial attacks on Iraq in 2003, the Americans did not learn from what they failed to recognise in 1990. They also privileged what they acquired electronically over cultural knowledge of Iraqi society or of Saddam Hussein's government. In part, that was because they did not have the agents on the ground to give them human intelligence; instead, they relied on Iraqi exiles, who had been out of the country for too long. In part, too, it reflected an appetite for secret intelligence, fostered in both world wars, over open-source information. Secret services will prioritise an intercept over a newspaper report.

Today, however, the boundaries between intelligence services and open-source acquisition, and between the product of innovative technologies and human judgement, are becoming blurred. Much of the publicly available intelligence on Russian movements in eastern Ukraine has been acquired by independent, non-state bodies such as Bellingcat, the Netherlands-based investigative journalism group. Using open-source material, from the internet to mobile phones, it completed fine-grain analysis to show who shot down Malaysian Airlines flight MH17 on 17 July 2014. The amount of intelligence that is freely available swamps the capacities of human intelligence assessment. As a result, 'big data' is being analysed by artificial intelligence. The results carry significant implications for policymakers as well as for commanders in the field, but they do not remove the need for human judgement. One senior British officer tells a story of his time in Afghanistan, when photographic intelligence revealed evidence of Afghans working the ground overnight, so prompting the conclusion – reinforced at daylight by clear signs of recently moved earth – that they had been burying improvised explosive devices (IEDs). They had not; they were tilling the ground while it was cool and irrigating it when the water could not evaporate too quickly. The questions asked of artificial intelligence, just like those posed of any other form of intelligence, will shape the conclusions that emerge. Intelligence in war is as much an art as a science, as much a product of common sense as of technical brilliance. Wrong questions and false assumptions are just as likely to produce errors in the application of intelligence today as they were in the past.

Bockdruckerye te Haerlem gevonden ontrent het Jaer 1440

Wat is de Druckery een konst wel hoog te roemen!
En wat is Haerlem ook wel over-waerd te noemen!
P. Zaenredam. Inuent.   O edele wyse Stad, die dese konst eerst vond!   J. v. Velde. sculpsit.
Wat schort hier Mentz de neus? Die segge, snoert den mond.

Etching depicting a prints hop in Haarlem in the
1440s, Jan van de Velde (II) after Pieter Jansz
Saenredam, 1626–1628.

THE WAR AGAINST PRINTING

Alexander Lee

'The pen is a virgin,' wrote Filippo de Strata in the late fifteenth century, but 'the printing press is a whore.' And that wasn't the half of it. Born into a wealthy Pavian family, Filippo had joined the Dominican Order at a young age and had spent most of his adult life at the convent of San Cipriano, on the Venetian island of Murano. One of the smallest religious communities in the lagoon, it could boast no special intellectual renown, yet its members still attached great importance to the production of manuscripts, and Filippo was no exception. He translated texts from Latin into Italian, copied sermons and biblical commentaries, and even penned a few works of his own. Yet he was also a pompous, even arrogant man, who seemed to be at war with the world around him. His invectives were legion. He attacked the French for spreading heresy among unsuspecting Italians and wrote a rather clunky elegy against the use of organ music in church. But it was printing which attracted the worst of his ire. In a Latin address to Doge Nicolò Marcello, written at some point between August 1473 and December 1474, and in a vernacular poem composed about 20 years later, he lashed out at it with unconcealed hatred. He not only called the press a 'whore', but also accused printers of being 'asses' – and even asked the Doge to ban printing altogether.

It was, perhaps, not the most obvious of targets. Between the development of the first writing systems in ancient Mesopotamia and the dawn of the internet age, nothing so revolutionised communication as the invention of printing by Johannes Gutenberg (*c.*1400–68). Indeed, as the English statesman and philosopher Francis Bacon (1561–1626) later wrote, it was one of the three innovations 'unknown to the ancients' which could genuinely be said to have 'changed the appearance of the whole world'.

Granted, the idea behind it wasn't *completely* new. For some time, Europeans frustrated by traditional forms of scribal production had been looking for ways of speeding things up. Back in the thirteenth century, the so-called *pecia* system had been introduced at the universities of Oxford, Paris and Bologna. Books which were in high demand were divided up into sections and rented out a piece at a time, so that several students could copy the same text simultaneously. A little over 100 years later, some Rhenish or Burgundian carvers may also have experimented with printing very short texts using wooden blocks. But even at their best, such methods were clumsy, expensive and fraught with problems.

What made Gutenberg's innovation so remarkable was his use of movable metal type. This not only allowed compositors to set any text, but it was also so durable that it could be used hundreds – if not thousands – of times without any significant loss of clarity. Combined with a press (modelled on that used for producing wine), a stickier variety of ink and large sheets of paper, Gutenberg's type allowed a printer to produce books in greater numbers and more quickly than anyone had ever thought possible. As the humanist Benedetto Brugnoli (1427–1502) later observed, 'twenty men may [now] print in a month more books than one hundred could previously have copied in a year.'

After Gutenberg established his press in Mainz in *c*.1450, printing spread rapidly – if rather erratically – throughout Europe. Within less than 20 years, presses had been established in Bamberg, Strasbourg, Cologne, Subiaco, Basel, Rome, Augsburg, Nuremberg and perhaps elsewhere too. As Giorgio Merula (*c*.1430–94) noted, this was thanks largely to printers from 'that once rugged and brutish land of Germany', who had either set off in search of somewhere to establish their own presses or who had been actively headhunted by foreign rulers.

Venice was something of a latecomer. Not until 1469 did the French printer Nicolas Jenson (*c*.1420–80) found the first press in the city. That it had taken so long is perhaps surprising. Then at the zenith of its 'imperial age', Venice was arguably the most important commercial entrepôt in Europe and had particularly strong trading links with Germany. No less importantly, it could also boast an intellectual standing which few could rival. But having acquired the new technology, it quickly made up for lost time. By the time Filippo de Strata wrote his first polemic against printing, in 1473 or 1474, the city was already 'stuffed with books'. In just five years, no fewer than 176 different editions had appeared. By 1480, that number would rise to 593; and it has been estimated that, by 1500, more than 4,000 editions had been published by almost 150 different presses – twice as many as Paris, its nearest competitor, and accounting for 13 to 14% of all the books published in the whole of Europe.

Venetian presses did not have it easy, though. Although Desiderius Erasmus (1466–1536) once tartly noted that it was easier to become a printer than a baker, it required a great deal of specialist equipment – and even more investment. Presses, it was true, were relatively cheap; but a type font could be extremely expensive, while the costs of labour and paper were positively eye-watering. Given that each edition was generally produced in advance of demand, this made the whole enterprise extremely risky. If too many books were printed, or a sudden economic downturn caused a contraction in the market, a press could find itself staring bankruptcy in the face, as many did in the great crisis of 1472–73. One way of minimising the risk was specialisation. While works of classical literature tended to be popular with educated readers, religious and legal texts were a more reliable source of income. But even in these fields, there were no guarantees. In the absence of copyright protection, there was nothing to stop one printer from pinching the proofs of a new work from a rival and rushing out a pirated version before it could be published. It is hardly surprising that, of the 100 or so printing houses operating in Venice up to 1490, only 23 were active in the following decade, and just ten survived the century.

Nor did printing completely supplant scribal production. Quite the reverse, in fact. Even decades after the foundation of the first presses, manuscripts were still being commissioned, and scribes were still much in demand. Some people – such as the Florentine bookseller Vespasiano da Bisticci (1421–98) or the bibliophile Federico da Montefeltro (1422–82) – actually preferred manuscripts, both for their beauty and for their extremely high value. Precisely because printing was such a risky business, there was also some crossover between the practices. The Cretan scribe Zacharias Callierges (c.1473-c.1524), for example, abandoned his pen to become a printer, only to take it up again when his press collapsed. As with all great innovations, the market took time to adjust; and there was as much uncertainty about the future as there was continuity with the past.

Yet however uncertain the fate of presses or incomplete the replacement of manuscript culture, the shock of printing was profound. As the historian Martin Lowry noted, it 'must have been both a traumatic and an exhilarating experience'. All that seemed familiar was abruptly thrown into confusion. And as people scrambled to adapt to the sudden availability of books, it was only natural that questions were also raised about the wider social implications of the new technology.

For many, printing was an overwhelmingly positive innovation. Almost as soon as the first presses were established in Italy, learned men rushed to sing its praises. To some, in fact, it seemed almost divine. In 1468, the bishop of Aleria, Giovanni Andrea de Bussi (1417–75), hailed it as a 'holy art' (*sancta ars*). Three years later, the Venetian doctor Nicolaus Gupalatinus wrote that it was a 'miracle unheard of in all previous ages'. And in 1489, Guiniforte Boccaccino of Pavia went so far as to claim that humanity owed as much to the inventors of printing as to those who figured out how to bake bread.

One of its principal attractions was that it had the potential to democratise knowledge. In the past, the high cost of manuscripts had meant that only the well-to-do could afford them. Now that books could be produced in large numbers, however, printed volumes could be sold for much lower prices, making them available to those of lesser means for the first time. As Bussi remarked, it was possible for even the poorest to build a library of his own and for learning to become accessible to all. Excited by the prospect, some of those associated with presses began writing texts explicitly targeted at furthering the spread of knowledge. In 1483, for example, Fra Iacopo Filippo Foresti of Bergamo (1434–1520) published his *Supplementum chronicarum*. A sort of 'bluffers' guide' to world history, this was expressly designed to make available to the masses knowledge which had previously been restricted only to the few.

As many observers recognised, this had a range of knock-on benefits. For some, the most important of these was permanence was the foremost of these. According to the Florentine humanist Bartolomeo della Fonte (1446–1513), printers could 'confer eternity' on whatever they produced. Since printing put more books into circulation, he reasoned, it would ensure that ancient texts were less likely to be lost, and it would crown modern authors with certain fame. Others believed that the 'flood' of new books would lead to moral enlightenment. There was some justification for this. Recent research into domestic life has revealed that books of hours were by far the most commonly owned texts; and, as Caroline Anderson has argued, the fact that these books were often kept in the *camera* (bedchamber/dayroom) suggests that they were read on a daily basis, including by women. It was hence only reasonable to assume that, as printing spread, so virtue would also grow. For the Franciscan friar Bernardino da Feltre (1439-94), God had shed 'so much light on these most wretched and dark times' through print that there was no longer any excuse for sin at all.

But not everyone was so enthusiastic. Others, for whom novelty and progress were far from synonymous, regarded printing with open hostility. Of these, none was more vehement than Filippo de Strata.

Like many of his contemporaries, he did not have any particular objection to books as physical objects. Although he is almost certain to have preferred manuscripts, he does not seem to have thought that printed works were, in themselves, unworthy of being read. Printers, however, were another matter. Much like his contemporary, the historian Marcantonio Sabellico (1436–1506), he reviled them as much for their 'plebeian' ways as for their foreign origins. To his mind, they were beggars and thieves who had no appetite for work but were always hungry for money. They had come to Italy, babbling in that ugly language of theirs, with no other goal than to put scribes out of a job. What was worse, they had no sense of propriety either. Drunk on strong wine and success, they were hawking books to every Tom, Dick and Harry. In doing so, they were not democratising learning – as Bussi and Foresti liked to believe – but debasing it. Whereas, in the past, the expense and scarcity of manuscripts had ensured that great care was always taken over the preparation of texts, the ease with which books could now be printed – coupled with the intense competition between presses – had led to all manner of rubbish being churned out. These days, Filippo argued, you could hardly open a volume without it being festooned with errors. This clearly did immense damage both to classical scholarship and to education. By putting such defective texts into the hands of the masses, he claimed, even those who could barely speak the vernacular would feel qualified to teach Latin. But since printers were interested only in making a quick buck off such 'unlettered' fools, they had no incentive to do any better. All that mattered was getting a new edition on the market as quickly as possible, irrespective of its quality.

For much the same reason, Filippo also believed that printing was a threat to public morality. If printers had sold nothing but religious works, it might not have been so bad; but because they were interested only in profit, they were trying to attract new readers by appealing to their baser instincts. All manner of bawdy and unsuitable volumes were being produced: from the torrid love poetry of Tibullus and Ovid, to the worst kind of modern filth. Given how cheaply such books were sold, it was inevitable that vice, rather than virtue, would flourish.

That the religious works printers did produce were of such poor quality only made the danger more acute. Previously, Filippo observed, the inaccessibility of the Bible and other devotional works helped keep the common people on the straight and narrow. Unable to understand the Latin language, they relied on priests to explain the meaning of scripture and the practices appropriate to a Christian life. But now that the Bible was appearing in crude Italian translations and hackneyed guides to the 'good life' were hitting the market, even the most ignorant might might feel emboldened to try interpreting God's words for themselves. As such, there was serious risk that honest folk would be led far from the path of orthodoxy. It was for this reason that Filippo characterised printing as a 'whore' (*meretrix*) – and called on Doge Marcello to banish it from Venice for ever.

As Martin Lowry noted, it is perhaps tempting to dismiss Filippo as a throwback – 'the last survivor of a doomed generation, screaming in the faces of a solid phalanx of noblemen, intellectuals, and artisans who march shoulder to shoulder towards enlightenment and a better life'. But this would do him a disservice. He was far from alone in his views. Many shared his scepticism of printing. Indeed, so new was the technology, and so rapidly was its landscape changing, that even those who could see some advantages were alarmed by its risks. In 1481, for example, Gerolamo Squarzafico (*fl.* 1471–1503) wrote a letter purporting to be from the late Francesco Filelfo (1398–1481), in which he lamented the illiteracy of printers. So too Giorgio Merula, had doubts about whether printing would have a positive or negative effect on classical scholarship. And in 1470, the Florentine humanist Niccolò Perotti (1429–80) even asserted that the books then in circulation were so inaccurate that it would have been better they had never been printed.

Though such concerns sometimes tended towards the hysterical, they were grounded less in hope than in reality. With certain notable exceptions, such as the printer-scholar Aldus Manutius (*c.*1450–1515), printers did indeed turn out a lot of faulty editions of classical texts. To make matters worse, some of these even drove better versions off the market. Just two years before Filippo began writing his Latin polemic, a spectacularly inaccurate edition of Ovid's works by Francesco Dal Pozzo

(Puteolanus, d.1490) was printed in Bologna. It deserved to be quickly forgotten; but because it was the first such edition of the poet's works (the so-called *editio princeps*), it was treated as if it were some gift from heaven – and a far superior version, published in Rome just a few months later, was consigned to oblivion. Whether printing corrupted public morals is, perhaps, open to question. While the Venetian Senate was not above banning, or even burning, some works for the sake of civic decency, we should be wary of taking the complaints of certain prelates too literally. Yet there can be no denying that printing *did* contribute to the spread of heterodoxy and was later instrumental in the dissemination of Reformation thought.

However distasteful a character Filippo de Strata may seem, his polemics against printing hence serve to illustrate that, amid the fog of change, the line between progress and peril can appear blurred, even to the most keen-eyed observer. It is perhaps just as well that, in this case, wishful thinking prevailed over unpleasant, if not unjustified, fears.

A crowd points to a UFO flying over the
Chrysler Building in New York, 1951.

IT CAME FROM OUTER SPACE

Tim Jenkins

The much-anticipated release in June 2021 of a US government report about unidentified flying objects – or 'Unidentified Aerial Phenomena' (UAPs), as they are termed in the publication – may, on the surface at least, have brought UFOs out of the realm of science fiction and into the arena of mainstream science.

As well as the report, ordered by Congress, military films of various incidents of UAPs were released. The report concludes that while objects have been seen, there is no evidence for (nor against) these being of extra-terrestrial provenance. This combination of elements – aerial sightings, political interest for defence reasons, the possibility of unearthly origins, raised but neither endorsed nor quashed – has been repeated at intervals during the last 70 years. The pattern remains remarkably constant, both in the form of the question – are these UFOs from another planet? – and in the lack of any clear answer, for there is no incontrovertible evidence on either side of the debate.

In an unresolved puzzle of this enduring kind, we might ask about the categories in which the question is posed: what kind of thinking allows the problem to be termed in the way it has, and when did it come into existence? What allows us to think in terms of UFOs and their possibility or impossibility?

The crux lies in the changes associated with new forms of media. A series of new technologies, dating from the end of the nineteenth century and extending to the present, have permitted new experiences and new forms of imagination. The gramophone, for example, allows the experience of being addressed directly by an absent person, even a dead person. Radio, a later development, though not by much, permits us to hear disembodied voices from far away. Both, initially, had an uncanny quality; they abolished differences of time and space. Photographs, likewise, made present images of elsewhere, never encountered in experience, or brought before us images of people we may have known, even loved, but who had lives in other places. And motion pictures multiply novelties of these kinds: they not only present records of stretches of other times and places, but – through recording and replaying – create new perspectives and new angles on scenes, not only allowing new things to be seen but fresh details to emerge, reframing incidents, calling attention to hitherto unperceived moments of significance, and presenting short sequences that may alter the meaning of an encounter. In short, we might say that new media create new kinds of experience and possibilities, and turn our lives into new sorts of narratives.

New media have always had this kind of effect. But the means of recording, storage and replaying – developed from the 1880s on – were particularly striking both in their effects and in the widespread nature of their impact, touching not simply an elite few but almost everyone, through radio and cinema, altering the nature of experience and memory, creating new shared ways of being in the world. As a population, we perceive everyday life in categories that derive from these experiences, these vivid enactments of things that are not there. The world in which we live has changed, and these new ways of grasping life as it is lived operate at several levels. For instance, we anticipate the sudden presence of minds from elsewhere; we can receive direct communication from absent friends; we can conceive of new perspectives on situations, modelled often on shots from above that reveal patterns of behaviour or shots from below that reveal relations of power, and, most of all, we can conceive of ourselves as caught up in stories, or being touched by other stories, unknown to us but going on in the same space. Our life is, to a degree, cinematic, shaped by audiovisual images. And once collectively we have glimpsed the power of media in this regard, we can conceive of the world as being ordered by codes, and can imagine it is constructed by invisible means and controlled by unknown people whose intentions are hidden from us. A world shaped by experience of film is also, potentially, a paranoid world.

Flying saucers are a small feature of the imaginative space created within these new technological frames. They can be dated quite precisely: spaceships appear in fiction contemporarily with the development of radio and, like radio waves, travel through space, hiding their origin. The motives behind the appearance of spaceships are also often hidden – they make unexpected contact, and convey messages with implications that are hard to evaluate. These ideas were elaborated in early science fiction, a branch of pulp publishing popularised in the first half of the twentieth century, which drew on theosophical speculations for many of its details, describing spirit forms travelling between planets, organising cosmic evolution and aiding the development of the human race. These works offered a meditation on the contemporary human condition, confronted with the expansion of scientific knowledge and of the technology that accompanied it, and laid down most of the ground rules that apply in modern UFO sightings. In this fashion, science fiction provided content for a form arising independently.

But flying saucers only became a reality in the context of the Second World War and its transmutation into the Cold War; they coexisted with the extraordinary acceleration of technological development associated with the notion of 'total war', with the invention of atomic weapons, rocketry and supersonic flight, together with a range of other industries, including those concerned with communications – radio, radar and the rapid transmission and analysis of information through what became known as information technology. Weapons and communications form a single complex and define the modern world we still precariously inhabit.

When they first appeared in the late 1940s, flying saucers were an amalgam of characteristics drawn from contemporary research projects – silent flight, radical circular designs, alternative power sources – and exhibited powers of manoeuvrability, acceleration and hovering that resembled images on screen, and showed evidence of interest in human military and industrial sites, with sightings concentrated around military testing grounds, nuclear stations, electrical plants and so forth. They were of interest to military intelligence and, since many of the sightings of daytime objects or night-time lights were by United States Air Force pilots, a unit was set up by the Air Force (newly separated from the Army) in 1947, a small part of the intelligence operation concerned with the properties of new enemy aircraft. This unit had a varied history, only being reabsorbed into other projects in 1968. Its concerns were precisely those of the recent report to Congress.

The report looks at recent sightings of UAPs – fast-moving objects filmed by aircraft or from naval vessels, objects which show extraordinary manoeuvrability and which exhibit intelligent behaviour, apparently investigating ships and accelerating away when approached by aircraft, shooting into the sky or, sometimes, plunging into the sea. The question of their origin is an important one: they might be supersonic weapons systems produced by other countries, yet their performance appears vastly advanced and beyond any known technology, with acceleration and deceleration powers that would destroy any human pilot. Discussions of the report have led to renewed theorising about potential interstellar origins, possible life-bearing planets in other solar systems, the conditions for development of other technological civilisations on such planets, and speculation concerning projects of observation and communication carried out by artificial intelligence – robots perhaps launched thousands of years ago but capable of undertaking research in our locality and in real time. The report, however, is far more circumspect, confining itself to reviewing the evidence but eschewing conclusions about extraterrestrial origins.

All this discussion shows an underlying concern not only with technological innovation – the latest military hardware and developments in information technology, not to mention the findings of radio astronomy – but also with a certain conception of communication, understood as the central characteristic of intention and therefore of intelligent life, human or otherwise. Communication is understood in this sense: that ideas may be conveyed without distortion or interruption between minds – effectively a bodiless voice speaking straight to the receiver's ear, for which radio offers a model. This idea is far older than the Second World War, but it takes a new form in the late 1940s, linked with the appearance of the technical concept of 'information' emerging from considerations concerning transmission of signals and encrypting (and decoding) messages.

In practice, conveying precise information in an undistorted form over distances is only a small part of complex common enterprises, whether in war or peacetime. But in the post-war period, the concept of information has come to be considered a sufficient key to describe all kinds of processes, in nature and in every aspect of human activity: not only genetics and cell biology, but economics, diplomacy, social life, personal relations and therapy have all been expressed in terms of the unimpeded exchange of information. And using this concept, the communication of information from one mind to another has been central to imagining the purposes and actions of visitors from other planets. Speculation concerning their aims in showing themselves, their possible agenda, what they might be seeking to exchange, and our anticipation of the appropriate forms of contact (the search for signals, construing and constructing alien languages), are all cast in terms of the exchange of information. Without the concept of information and the ambition of its pure (bodiless) communication, we would have no frame within which to make sense of our hopes of encounter.

Although it appears to take us some way from the content of the recent Congress report – unidentified objects seen, defence concerns, the source(s) of the objects in question – it is worth adding that 'information', which is a structuring concern of the report, links up with a particular understanding of 'memory'. This is memory conceived as the retention of accurate information; the recovery of a particular significant encounter in the past and therefore an accurate record retained with all its significance intact, capable of being relived and explored in full. This is memory as film. This idea is vital for the potential memory recovery in alien abduction cases, but it is also needed to give character and purpose to the possible alien visitors, who may be future forms of life derived from the human race, bearing an understanding of the past (which for us means our future history), and so are able to help guide us through threats and crises. Again, although the idea of memory has a long history, the concept only gained its present possibilities, that of access to accurate and complete records, recently, with new recording technologies and the focus on the ideal of transparent communication of information between minds. Hence the play with artificial intelligence in satellites, monitoring us and, perhaps, relaying information home.

The basic materials, then, for understanding the continuing life of sightings of unidentified flying objects are these. First, the close mutual implication of weapons technology and media images, together with the taking up in these images of theosophical ideas, transmitted through science fiction, of minds 'out there' concerned with human contributions to cosmic evolution. Then, an over-reliance on the ideal of direct communication between minds, taken up and elaborated in the idea that information constitutes a key to the intelligibility of the human and natural worlds alike. And last, a notion of memory as the recall of exact information. These three clusters of interrelated ideas have remained relatively constant, although developing, over the past 80 years. And once this complex was initiated, around the end of the Second World War, it was inevitable that something like flying saucers would make an appearance in a world exhausted by warfare, dominated by security concerns, and obliged to place its hope of survival in the continuous development of new and extraordinary technologies. The categories still generate UFO sightings of the kind that prompt questions: 'Are they true? Or error? Or fiction?' This creates accompanying dilemmas for politicians and strategists responsible for national security, providing material for experts, commentators and amateur speculators.

The formula has been put to work by the wider population; it has become key to popular thinking about the centrality of the military-industrial complex to American public life, whether in the ongoing role of media representations that simultaneously display some aspects of that centrality (NASA, for example) and occlude others (such as the Defense Advanced Research Projects Agency), or, more generally, in the play of information, memory and forgetting which appears both in widespread public distrust of the state and in a vast range of therapies, whether concerned with recovered memory or with clearing obstacles to communication with self or others. In short, this complex of ideas is well instantiated in the modern world, part of the fabric of our imagination, continually evolving but with certain constant features.

We shall not, then, cease to be confronted with reports of UFOs (or UAPs) and their unresolvable dilemmas until a profound shift occurs in the way in which we make sense of novelties of many kinds. Turning the theory on its head, the continuing, if also mutating, life of flying saucers offers a reliable clue to central questions about the world in which we find ourselves.

Neo-Assyrian cylinder seal with a cultic scene,
ca. 911–612 BCE.

TECHNOLOGY TRANSFER ACROSS THE AGES

Daniel T. Potts

It is a truism to say that technology is all around us. Whether it's the mobile phone you reach for before getting out of bed, the electricity powering your home, the car, bus or train you take to work or the web interface you use to attend a meeting, teach a class or consult with your doctor, technology is literally staring you in the face, all day, every day. Ah, you think, but not if I live off-grid. If I'm in a cabin in the forest without electricity, running water and Wi-Fi, then I'm free from technology. Actually, you're not. The axe you use to split wood, the bucket and rope you employ to acquire water, the boots on your feet, the spun fabrics of which your clothes are made, are all products of technology.

Philosophers, historians, artists, scientists and engineers, ranging from the ultra-theoretical to those with a string of patents to their name, have written about technology for centuries, and the definition of this vast, often nebulous term has had countless incarnations since Aristotle's writings on *techne*. As a domain of knowledge, he argued, *techne* enjoyed a lower status than either theoretical or moral knowledge, a point that was not lost on Eric Schatzberg in his recent book *Technology: Critical History of a Concept*. That perspective has certainly resonated throughout much of Western scholarship and has permeated my own field of ancient Near Eastern studies since the nineteenth century.

Writing about irrigation, metallurgy, ceramic manufacture or fishing nets has unquestionably been seen as a lower-status form of scholarship than expounding upon Gilgamesh, the law code of Hammurabi or royal rhetoric. And yet, as in our twenty-first-century world, technology was everywhere in the ancient Near East and, as such, is every bit as deserving of serious study as literature, art, hermeneutics or semiotics. For while Aristotle may have written a good deal about *techne*, the Greeks certainly did not invent technology, and although I have no interest in joining the late Samuel Noah Kramer in extolling the 'firsts' of Mesopotamian civilisation and their resonance for us today, it is certainly the case that technology predates ancient Greece by several million years, beginning with the first modification of matter by early hominins.

Technology today can be identified on many different scales, from the nano to the mega. In the ancient Near East, the scale was more compressed, yet the same principle obtained. Just as technology aids us – complicating our lives as well, to be sure, and placing constraints on what we can and cannot do – it also performed that function in antiquity. Technology in the ancient Near East can be discerned operating at a variety of physical and spatial scales, along a spectrum extending from the micro to the macro. At the micro end of the technological spectrum we can, for example, identify the use of boring and cutting tools to manufacture cylinder seals, small cylinders of a hard material (baked clay, shell, stone, metal) only a few centimetres long, engraved with scenes and sometimes inscriptions (in mirror-writing) which, when rolled onto a soft surface, like an unbaked clay tablet or lump of clay sealing the mouth of a storage jar, left an impression of whatever was carved on the seal itself as a means of identification. Thousands upon thousands of such cylinder seals, the earliest of which date to *c.*3500 BC and the latest to *c.*300 BC, are scattered across museums and private collections around the world. As for macro-scale examples of technology, these included buildings standing tens of metres high and extending over many thousands of square metres, irrigation canals running for kilometres, brickyards producing millions of baked bricks each year, state-run pottery workshops where hundreds of thousands of ceramic vessels were thrown on fast wheels and fired in industrial-sized kilns, and textile factories employing tens of thousands of workers (mainly women and children) that turned out hundreds of thousands of pieces of cloth for the dependent workers employed by the central government.

Writing, a technology that transformed communication and became an instrument of accounting long before any prayers or epics were recorded, was invented in southern Mesopotamia *c.*3400 BC and, over the ensuing centuries, became an essential part of administration and governance for both small states and large empires, employed for everything from small receipts for sales of goods and services to royal propaganda. Archaeologists and scholars of early writing systems have often discussed the 'idea of writing' and the problem of independent invention. In effect, this is a subject that applies to all technology in the ancient Near East. Was writing invented only once, after which the knowledge of it, from scribal practices to concepts about how to deploy it, diffused widely across the Eurasian landmass? Or were different writing systems invented in different areas that had no contact with or influence upon one another? Precisely the same discussion has taken place among metallurgists. Was bronze, for example, the alloy of tin and copper, discovered and perfected in far-flung locales, ranging from western Europe to China, or was it a unique invention, the knowledge of which spread across the continents?

In trying to assess the likelihood of prehistoric technology transfer there are, of course, many considerations. Bronze, for example, came to be employed in many areas lacking in tin or copper sources. In such cases, it was not necessarily a knowledge of the mining and refining (smelting) of ores that was adopted from another regional centre, but of casting and methods of manufacture. This raises the question of technological knowledge, or know-how. Is it possible for complex technologies that may involve what could be called 'folk chemistry' – the control of oxygen supply in a furnace, the use of fluxes and so on – to spread through verbal means? As we have no evidence of the movement of anything resembling written instructions or handbooks on technologies such as smelting, refining, casting or the construction and use of kilns, is it conceivable that such technological complexes were communicated and diffused without an actual movement of trained craftsmen?

There are countless instances throughout history of what could be called intellectual property theft – from the appropriation of the technology of Chinese silk manufacture in Byzantium to beer-brewing or porcelain recipes in Europe. When archaeological evidence clearly demonstrates that, chronologically, a certain technological innovation occurred in one place and, a thousand years later, it is found in another, distant locale, we are certainly justified in positing the origin of the technology in one core area and its subsequent diffusion elsewhere. Whether we are talking about bronze, which appeared in the Near East long before it began to be made in China, or cotton, which is attested in India millennia before it appeared in the Near East, most scholars are comfortable with presuming that one area was an original hearth of invention from which a given technology spread to other parts of Eurasia. The question is, however, by what means?

Itinerant craftsmen are well evidenced in the ancient Near East and one can conjure up any number of scenarios that might help us understand how their movement resulted in the concomitant spread of a particular technology. Gold filigree, for instance, was present in Georgia long before examples of it appear in the Royal Cemetery of Ur in southern Mesopotamia, *c.*2500 BC. Could some craftsmen have found their way from the Caucasus to what is today southern Iraq, introducing a new technology in jewellery manufacture for an élite clientele? The likelihood of this happening over vast distances within the lifetime of a single crafts-man seems slim. However, the time-honoured, if somewhat discredited, notion of 'diffusion', once a panacea for all the inexplicable, seemingly coeval appearances of technologies across Eurasia, has something to offer in cases such as these. In the past, prehistorians rejected diffusion because it was invoked as a mechanism of contact in ways that now seem somewhat laughable. Every time the same motif appeared on pottery found thousands of kilometres apart, it was attributed to diffusion, going in the direction from the earlier to the later manifestation of the design. In the case of some technologies, critics of diffusionism argued, it was more logical to assume independent invention in two or more different places, rather than a speculative, chronologically implausible case of diffusion.

In fact, there are other ways in which technologies may diffuse and people, including craftsmen, may move across the landscape. Already in prehistoric times the presence of hugely dissimilar, painted pottery in one and the same small settlement suggests that exogamy may have served as a mechanism for the diffusion of alien motifs and even technologies. If, as has been demonstrated in ethnographic studies conducted all over the world, most pre-modern, pre-industrialised pottery manufacture was done by women, and exogamous marriage combined with patrilocal resi-dence patterns were in place – in other words, women from one village, when they married, moved to the village of their husband – then it is easy to see how decorative motifs, and even shapes and pottery production techniques, could have been brought from one place to another as female potters were transplanted from their home villages to those of their mates.

Pottery manufacture and pottery decoration are not the only techno-logies that may have been transmitted across the landscape in this fash-ion. Metallurgy, stoneworking, textile crafts – anything, in short, from the macro to the micro – could have been diffused through exogamous marriage patterns. Of course, there are other driving factors as well. The advantages of a technology have, historically, led rulers to engage skilled craftsmen from outside their native regions. Examples abound in more recent times of skilled jewellers, armourers, fortification specialists, astrologers, physicians and many others leaving their homes to work for foreign princes. The advantages of cast bronze weaponry that could be standardised and mass-produced (within reason) would have been apparent to the kings of the city states of Umma and Lagash in southern Iraq when they went to war with each other in the mid-third millennium BC. Spearheads with sockets that could be firmly attached to a wooden spear shaft, cast iron arrowheads with three projecting wings for better flight and penetration, and armour-piercing war hammers were probably not invented over and over again, but, as technologies to be employed in war, conferring advantages to those with them over those without, they were almost certainly diffused along with the metalsmiths capable of manufacturing them.

In all of these examples we must reckon with a sliding archaeological timescale, from the earliest attestation of a given technology to the later manifestations of it. Yet such diffusion need not have occurred overnight. In some cases, it was surely an incremental process by which technologies and the advantages they brought with them were carried across short distances, through adjacent polities, until, after a few centuries or a millennium, they were to be found in widely separated areas, geographically speaking. In this sense, diffusion is a perfectly respectable mechanism to invoke in studies of technology transfer.

Yet another issue that is rarely mentioned in studies of technology in the ancient Near East is that of different states of technological sophistication in different areas. Technologies serve us in a variety of ways and can become essential without our even realising it. But not all societies or their members have the same technological needs. The military, for example, as noted in the examples cited above, had an appetite for certain kinds of technology that differed from the members of a village community. Urban societies had needs that rural ones did not. From an archaeological perspective, these differing needs contributed to a very different material culture 'signature'. In other words, the sorts of finds made in excavating an urban setting may differ from those found in a rural one. A rural community may appear 'Neolithic' compared to an urban one. Two contemporaneous sites – one urban and the other rural – may differ to such an extent that the rural one appears stuck in the Stone Age while a few kilometres away people were living in utterly different conditions that appear more sophisticated and technologically advanced. This is not to cast aspersions on rural members of a society, for Neolithic societies, if by that we mean early agriculturalists and herders, used just as much technology as their Bronze or Iron Age urban-dwelling brethren. They simply used different technologies.

The very terms we employ to describe the broad phases of the human past in Eurasia – Stone Age, Bronze Age, Iron Age – are inherently technology-based. What the so-called three-age system (devised by the Christian Jürgensen Thomsen (1786–1865) c.1818 as a means of organising the collection in the Oldnordisk Museum in Copenhagen) failed to capture was the simultaneity of different technological systems. It is now clear, however, thanks to absolute methods of dating like radiocarbon, that hunters, gatherers and farmers, using what might be termed Stone Age technologies, lived side by side with town and city dwellers making use of technologies that might be more commonly ascribed to the Bronze or Iron Age. It is also clear that, in some areas, bronze tools and weapons continued in use for centuries after some neighbouring regions had moved from bronze to iron for most of their needs, while other contemporary communities – hunters, gatherers, fishermen, farmers – may have continued to use flaked stone tools that, taken out of context and without reliable means for their dating, could easily be mistaken for objects of Palaeolithic type from the Stone Age, thousands of years older.

What we see, therefore, is abundant evidence of the contextually dependent adoption of technology in ancient Near Eastern societies. Communities living in proximity to each other may have used very different sorts of technology, giving the appearance that one was still in the Stone Age while another was more 'advanced'. The broad-brush approach, like Thomsen's three-age system, led to a layer cake image of unidirectional technology uptake that is far too simplistic. The explosion of archaeological exploration in the Near East since the Second World War has resulted in the acquisition of a wealth of data from what were once considered marginal or peripheral zones. In reality, the nineteenth- and early-twentieth-century focus on high-profile 'centres' of civilisation has given way to a much more truthful, accurate picture of life throughout the multiplicity of environmental zones that characterise the region. This picture shows us that humankind did not move in lockstep up an imaginary ladder of technological evolution. Technologies were adopted according to differing needs. Whether it was the proximity of abundant copper sources and the technical efficacy of bronze tools that caused the retention of bronze technology in the Persian Gulf, while contemporary communities in Assyria and Anatolia adopted iron, or the military imperative of Hittite and Egyptian armies that fuelled evolution in chariotry, technology was an independent variable in human existence that reflected the needs of the individuals, groups and communities employing it. What scholars have often labelled 'conservatism' with reference to technology – making a moral judgement upon those who seemingly shunned new technology out of a kind of ignorant or perverse unwillingness to change – can be shown to reflect a deep understanding of exactly what a given technology does and why it is implemented. Change and innovation in ancient technology are abundantly attested and so, too, is continuity. Technological praxis, learned experience and centuries-long tradition are all entwined in strategies of technological deployment in ancient societies that we, as modern students of those societies, must seek to understand, not to judge.

Illustration of the Antikythera mechanism.
Front and rear views are at left and centre,
with an exploded view at right.

ANCIENT CREATIONS: FROM THE ANTIKYTHERA MECHANISM TO WESTERN MUSIC

Armand D'Angour

In 1901 an extraordinary object was discovered in an ancient Roman shipwreck (dating to around 70 BC) off the Greek island of Antiky-thera. Now displayed in the Athens National Museum, the so-called Antikythera Mechanism, an intricate treasure constructed in Sicily some centuries earlier, consisted of a complex design of gears and wheels, of which 82 heavily encrusted bronze fragments were recovered. The sheer number of convolutions of the instrument and its sad state of preservation have meant that work on reconstructing the true form of the original has taken more than a century since its discovery. Recently, however, it has become possible to explain how the mechanism worked and what its purpose was. Amazingly, its moving wheels and displays were designed to indicate the changing positions of stars far in advance, so that its users might be able to predict celestial phenomena such as solar and lunar eclipses, and obtain calendrical information to calculate the timing of future athletic events such as the Olympic Games.

The Antikythera Mechanism not only provides a detailed representation of the astronomical knowledge of the era, it is a *tour de force* of engineering. Although Greeks of the Hellenistic Age (323–33 BC) are known to have designed devices such as early astrolabes and steam-powered automata, nothing as complex as the Antikythera Mechanism was to be produced by human ingenuity for more than a thousand years. An object of this kind – perhaps this very one – was known to the Roman statesman and orator Cicero (first century BC). In his treatise *On the State*, Cicero has a speaker ascribe the creation of what he calls a 'globe' to the famous Greek scientist and inventor Archimedes, who had lived and worked in Syracuse, the foremost city in Sicily, in the third century BC:

> The Sicilian geometrician must have had a genius superior to any
> thing we imagine in human nature...his invention was amazing: he
> calculated how with a single turn one could make unequal and

different motions in different directions. [By moving the globe] one could track the relationship of the moon and sun using the same number of turns on the bronze device as the actual number of days. It showed the eclipse of the sun as one might see it in the sky, and the moon entering the earth's shadow.

Despite Cicero's detailed testimony to the existence of this invention, and even though the physical remains of the Antikythera Mechanism prove its operation, such an object remains a singularity in the known history of the ancient world. Where does innovation of this kind – or even innovation in general – fit into ancient thinking and experience? Throughout the centuries of antiquity, people passed their daily lives in much the same way as those before them had for millennia. They worshipped the gods of their ancestors, practised old-established social customs, ploughed their fields as had their forefathers, and fought wars face to face with their neighbours just as their predecessors had. This way of life survived for thousands of years after antiquity. The expression *longue durée*, the long time span, was coined by historians of the French Annales school to speak of the long-term historical structures that underlie the more oft-told story of rapidly changing events (*histoire événementielle*).

While it might be tempting to think that the Antikythera Mechanism was just the tip of an ancient technological iceberg, it is hard to substantiate such a view. While some attention was devoted to technology, innovation is most often found to have revolved around the creation of artillery weapons for the purpose of waging successful wars of conquest. Archimedes himself was known to be an exceptional inventor, as the designer of inventions such as the water-screw and the grappling hook, as the engineer of the giant ship *Syracusia*, and as the formulator of important mathematical principles and theorems. The evidence suggests that, with a few individual exceptions, the wider Greek world of the period, and indeed of the centuries prior and subsequent to Archimedes' time, had little interest in or engagement with scientific novelties. In fact, in the history of classical scholarship, the ancient Greeks have usually been charged with a disinclination to all kinds of change and novelty. They have even been described as living 'in the grip of the past' (the title of a 1953 book about Greek cultural attitudes) and positively averse to innovation of any kind.

It is surprising, however, that such a stark view of ancient Greek traditionalism held sway as long as it did. The earliest term for 'innovation' is found first in texts from fifth-century BC Athens, in the word *kainotomia*. While this originally connoted 'cutting a new vein' in mining for metallic ores, it was soon extended to the more conceptual and artistic forms of innovation in which Greeks excelled. The fact is that despite their alleged aversion to the new, the ancient Greeks have long been acclaimed as the creators – particularly over the archaic and classical periods spanning five centuries from 800 to 300 BC – of a wide range of hugely significant cultural innovations. Among these, the invention of alphabetic writing, money, empirical medicine, lifelike sculpture, architectural forms, drama and historical literature, and the formulations of logic, philosophy, mathematical proof and political thought, are regularly cited.

How could it be possible that such demonstrably innovative people as the ancient Greeks were averse to innovation? But equally, how could it be possible for an unquestionably traditional society, as by and large the Greeks and even the famously ingenious Athenians undoubtedly were, to come up with, foster and disseminate so many of the fundamentally novel disciplines, ideas and practices that are acknowledged to have originated with them? Numerous answers have been proposed to explain these apparent contradictions; and one answer must be that the circumstances in which the Greeks found themselves were particularly conducive to creativity.

For any kind of innovation to emerge and to be adopted, a key requirement is that favourable conditions – individual, social, or political – must prevail. The conditions for innovation include such things as the freedom to spend time thinking, an openness to different ideas and practices, the existence of incentives to innovate, the ability to take risks without fear of reprisal, and the wherewithal to disseminate and diffuse new ideas to a wide circle of recipients who are in a position to criticise and improve on their own and other's efforts. It is rare in the historical record for such a combination of circumstances to be found. The independent citizen-states (*poleis*) of classical Greece benefited from unprecedented intellectual and social freedoms, while absorbing influences from cultures such as Phoenicia in the east (from whose writing system the Greeks developed their alphabet, the forerunner of the Latin alphabet) and Egypt to the south (the inspiration for Greek sculptural and architectural developments). For a while at least, a set of ideal conditions for innovation appear to have prevailed in the world of ancient Greece.

The stimulus to innovate is also related to a recognition of the benefits of doing something new, together with an understanding of how one might do so. Such a recognition is evident in ancient Greek texts, particularly in the areas of literary, artistic and musical production. The latter discipline provides explicit examples of the promotion of the new, as found in some surviving lines of lyric verse sung by a singer-songwriter called Timotheus. Timotheus, a native of the city of Miletus, was the most avant-garde musical performer of the late fifth century BC. He defiantly states in one of his songs: 'I don't sing the old songs, my new songs are better.' Contemporary writings, as well as Timotheus's rhythmically complex surviving lyrics, give us a sense of how he set about delighting and scandalising audiences in Athens. Notorious for being a redhead as well as a lyre player and composer with a taste for sensation and drama, he gained huge fame and popularity by spearheading the ancient equivalent of a pop revolution.

In addition to the bold rhythmical experimentation that can be heard in his lyrics (rhythmical patterns embedded in Greek words can be read as metrical units), Timotheus created new melodic possibilities by augmenting the number of strings used on the standard concert lyre, the *kithara* (the word from which 'guitar' derives). By combining this with use of a new lever mechanism (called *strobilos*) for altering the pitches of strings, he was also able to shift to melodies based around different tonal centres, modulating far more widely than performers who traditionally sang in a single key. The 'New Music', of which Timotheus was the foremost practitioner, had remarkably enduring appeal. The historian Polybius records that in this time (around 150 BC), boys in his native Arcadia (the central area of Greece's southern peninsula, the Peloponnese) learned the songs of Timotheus along with that of another 'new musician', Philoxenus, to perform in annual festivals. An inscription from Asia Minor records that devotees of Timotheus were still performing his music more than 500 years after his death.

The novel sounds and styles that Timotheus employed and created laid the groundwork for the kinds of melodies and harmonies that filled people's ears in the Roman and Christian eras. These sounds and idioms were, in turn, inherited and further developed by creators of music – troubadours and love lyricists as well as psalmists and church musicians – throughout Europe during the Middle Ages and the Renaissance. Arguably, therefore, Timotheus's innovations might be thought to form some of the earliest examples of what was to become the European musical tradition. The details show an individual adapting against a known background – and, in this case, Timotheus sought to extend rhythmical, harmonic and melodic expressiveness by combining his musical ideas with novel technical initiatives and mechanical resources. The result demonstrated, to the displeasure of conservative observers such as the philosopher Plato, a deliberate challenge to and reversal of existing norms of musical sobriety and simplicity.

We thus see that three mechanisms of innovation might be derived from this example of musical inventiveness – *adaptation, cross-fertilisation* and *reversal*. These fundamental principles may be found, singly and in combination, in every kind of innovative endeavour. Together with the conditions that allow and foster the creation of novelty, they constitute what might be called the roots of new creation.

The formulation of an idea of 'the roots of creation' is first found in the philosophy of a Greek thinker who lived two centuries before Archimedes. In the early fifth century, Empedocles of Acragas (modern Agrigento in Sicily) built on philosophical predecessors to challenge sixth-century thinkers, such as Thales and Anaximenes (both from Timotheus's native city, Miletus), who had argued that the universe arose from a single "originating principle' (*archê*) such as water or air. Empedocles proposed that there were four eternal roots of the physical cosmos: earth, fire, air and water. From the interchange of these elements, combining and separating through love and strife, the perceived universe arose. The roots themselves must be eternal, Empedocles argued; they could not have sprung into being from nothing.

The recognition that nothing new can arise without a pre-existing substrate is of great importance to the notion of innovation. It was to be stressed by the great fourth-century BC philosopher Aristotle in his analysis of change in the *Physics*. The proposition corrects a popular misapprehension of the meaning of 'radical' innovation, which is sometimes taken to mean 'new roots and all'. Such a thing, Aristotle insisted, cannot logically exist: what is new must have roots in the old. An innovation that was wholly unrelated to the past would simply be unrecognisable; so 'radical' innovation must properly mean 'new from the roots up'. Once this is recognised, various elements or mechanisms of innovation come into play, operating on the existing material to transform it – specifically the processes of adaptation, reversal and combination.

Greek antiquity is a rich source of stories that illustrate these processes, employed both deliberately and unconsciously. They serve to explain how the Greeks became notable innovators. The 'invention' of the alphabet, for instance, adapted from the letter-symbols used by the Greeks' Eastern neighbours, the Phoenicians, was not so much an invention as a cultural adaptation of great significance which allowed Greeks to commit their own ideas to writing using 24 phonetic symbols. The Phoenicians had named their 'a' after '*alif*', meaning 'ox' – the shape of the letter showing the pointed nose of the ploughing animal ahead, with the horns trailing behind – and the Greeks formalised the shape as their a[lpha]; similarly, they adapted Phoenician '*bet*' (house), the plan of a house with two rooms, to make their b[eta]; and so on for the whole alphabet.

Another overseas people, the Egyptians, were the inspiration for the earliest Greek representational statues of the sixth century BC. These initially followed the rigid style and contours of their models. But by combining sculptural techniques with an understanding of muscles and sinews as regularly viewed in athletic games, and informed by surgical practices developed to treat those wounded in battle, Greek sculptors transformed their statues into the fluid lifelike figures familiar from fifth-century Greek art.

The battlefield connection provides a further illustrative tale of innovation. Ancient battles between city states tended to follow a predictable pattern, with the strongest fighters stationed on the right wing of the phalanx. Once this column broke through their opponents, the battle was won, and the highly trained Spartans seemed invincible in such encounters. In 371 BC, however, at the Battle of Leuctra, the Theban commander Epaminondas reversed the standard procedure by putting his best fighters, reinforced by a column 50 men deep, on the left wing. The toughest of Spartans could make no headway, and their army, though much larger than that of the Thebans, was thrown into confusion. Epaminondas became master of the field through this simple reversal of the usual practice.

The intellectual and technical roots of the Antikythera Mechanism are lost to the historical record, but history records the Eureka moment of Archimedes, which may have resulted from his solution to the question of why a colossal ship (which he was commissioned to produce by the tyrant of Syracuse) should be able to float: that is, his formulation of the Archimedes principle. That story demonstrates a condition of innovation familiar to individual thinkers and inventors. Archimedes found his solution not at his desk or in front of his diagrams, but when he was relaxing in the bath.

Would-be innovators recognise the value not only of focusing intently on the problem in hand, but of taking time to switch off and allow a solution to emerge before immersing themselves once again in the intricate operation of making their solution work in practice. The mystifying questions raised by the existence of the remarkable Antikythera Mechanism seem likely to remain forever a mystery. But the conditions for intellectual illumination that the Archimedes Eureka story may demonstrate, as well as the other fundamental mechanisms and strategies that can be detected in so many stories of innovation from Greek antiquity, remain central to our understanding of how people and societies have come up with new ideas, and how we may continue to generate them.

Technicians working on the ENIAC machine,
1946 or later.

HOW THE INFORMATION AGE REALLY BEGAN

Ananyo Bhattacharya

Charles Babbage, Ada Lovelace and Alan Turing are all celebrated as computer pioneers, but the name of John von Neumann, a brilliant Hungarian-American mathematician once nearly as well known in America as Albert Einstein, is more likely to elicit blank looks than knowing nods. Yet, for all their genius, the origin of the information age that revolutionised the way we work and play can be traced much more directly to von Neumann than to any of these more famous figures.

That story begins with an accidental meeting on a train platform one summer evening in 1944 between von Neumann and Herman Goldstine, a fellow mathematician who had taught at the University of Michigan in peacetime but enlisted when the United States entered the Second World War. Goldstine was stationed at the Aberdeen Proving Ground, a weapons-testing facility in Maryland, where he was assigned to a team calculating artillery-firing tables – long lists of trajectory data showing how far shells fly under different conditions. He was waiting for his train home that day when he spotted von Neumann on the platform. Goldstine, who had attended some of von Neumann's lectures, recognised him instantly. He introduced himself, and the pair began to chat.

Von Neumann was 40 years old. A child prodigy born to a wealthy Jewish family in Budapest, he had published his first maths paper aged 17 and had a first draft of his PhD two years later. His thesis, published in 1925, had offered a solution to some deep problems in set theory that were baffling contemporary mathematicians, including Bertrand Russell, who were more than twice his age. A powerful tool for manipulating and proving theorems, set theory is the language of mathematics, so the young von Neumann's contribution to shoring up his discipline's foundations sealed his reputation as a mathematician of the first rank. Shortly afterwards, at the University of Göttingen, he rubbed shoulders with another boy wonder, Werner Heisenberg, who was busily laying the groundwork for a bewildering but successful new science of the atom and its constituents that was soon named 'quantum mechanics'. Von Neumann produced the first mathematically rigorous description of the new field in 1932, and one of the work's earliest fans would be a teenage Turing, who ordered the book in the original German as his prize for winning a school competition.

Lured to the US by Princeton University with the offer of a huge salary, von Neumann had arrived in January 1930 with his first wife and fellow Budapestian, Mariette Kövesi. Feeling that János – his Hungarian name – sounded too foreign in his new home, he urged American friends to call him 'Johnny'. Three years later, Johnny became one of the first professors to be hired by the elite new Institute for Advanced Study (IAS) in Princeton, along with Einstein. Aged 29, von Neumann was the youngest of the institute's recruits.

In America, convinced another world war was around the corner, and fearing European Jews would suffer a genocide as Armenians had under the Ottoman Empire, von Neumann made himself an expert in the mathematics of explosions. In demand by the American military and government, he was sent on a mission to wartime Britain in 1943, only to be recalled to the US by a letter from American physicist Robert Oppenheimer, begging him to join a 'somewhat Buck Rogers project' in Los Alamos, New Mexico. He joined the project, America's massive top-secret bid to build the atom bomb, and immediately made decisive contributions to the design of the 'implosion device', the more powerful weapon, which would eventually be detonated over Nagasaki. Shortly afterwards, von Neumann, who had a long-standing interest in comput- ing machines, began scouring the country to find ways to help Los Alamos tackle a long roll of bomb-related calculations. And that was when he bumped into Goldstine.

Von Neumann was nearly as renowned for his wit and a way with dirty limericks as for his near superhuman intellect. But when Goldstine told him that his role involved liaising with a team at the Moore School in Philadelphia who were busy building an electronic computer capable of more than 300 multiplications per second, von Neumann instantly turned serious. 'The whole atmosphere of our conversation changed,' Goldstine remembered, 'from one of relaxed good humour to one more like the oral examination for the doctor's degree in mathematics.'

The machine being built at the Moore School was the ENIAC

(Electronic Numerical Integrator and Computer), the brainchild of John W. Mauchly, a former physics teacher, and J. Presper Eckert, the whizz-kid son of a local real estate magnate who ran the teaching laboratory for the electronics course there. During the war, the task of computing artillery firing tables was consuming an evergrowing proportion of the Moore School's resources. The ENIAC had been commissioned to help clear the backlog.

The computer occupied a room that was roughly 30 feet wide and 56 feet long. Arrayed along the walls were the machine's innards: some 18,000 vacuum tubes, and banks of wiring and switches arranged in panels eight feet tall. But when von Neumann arrived on the scene in August 1944, the ENIAC, plagued by parts shortages, was still more than a year away from completion.

One of his first contributions to the project was to keep the army's money flowing in. He argued convincingly that the machine's usefulness would extend far beyond the purpose for which it had been designed. But from the moment he first saw it, von Neumann was thinking of a radically different kind of computer altogether. While the ENIAC was born as a machine of war, built for a single task, he understood that the future lay in a greatly more flexible device that could be easily reprogrammed. More importantly, von Neumann saw more clearly than anyone on the ENIAC team – and perhaps more clearly than anyone in the world – the best way to structure such a machine.

The result of his musings, First Draft of a Report on the EDVAC, would become the most influential document in the history of computing. 'Today, it is considered the birth certificate of modern computers,' says computer scientist Wolfgang Coy. Curiously, von Neumann was mentally prepared for this cutting-edge contribution to computing by his early abstruse mathematical work on set theory.

The problems in set theory that von Neumann had helped to address as a youth were part of the 'foundational crisis' which swept through mathematics during the early twentieth century. David Hilbert, the most eminent mathematician of the period, was troubled that his discipline seemed to be founded on shifting sands. 'If mathematical thinking is defective,' he asked, 'where are we to find truth and certitude?'

In 1928, he challenged his followers to ensure that the foundations of mathematics were secure once and for all. To do so, he said, they would need to demonstrate that mathematics is complete, consistent and decidable. By complete, Hilbert meant that all true mathematical theorems and statements can be proved from a finite set of assumptions or axioms. By consistent, he was demanding a proof that the axioms would not lead to any contradictions. The third of Hilbert's demands, that mathematics should be decidable, became widely known as the *Entscheidungsproblem* (decision problem): is there a step-by-step procedure – an algorithm – that can be used to show whether or not any particular mathematical statement can be proved? Mathematics would only be truly safe, said Hilbert, when, as he expected, all three of his demands were met.

Soon after Hilbert issued his challenge, the intellectually dynamic but psychologically frail Austrian mathematician Kurt Gödel would demonstrate that it is impossible to prove that mathematics is either complete or consistent. Five years after Gödel's breakthrough, a 23-year-old Turing would attack Hilbert's 'decision problem' in a way completely unanticipated by any other logician, conjuring up an imaginary machine to show that mathematics is not decidable.

Hilbert's quest for a perfectible mathematics ran aground. But he had forced mathematicians to think extremely rigorously about what can or cannot be proved. The systematic procedures they used to tackle Hilbert's challenges would soon become familiar – through von Neumann's work – in a very different guise, as computer programs.

To prove that maths was incomplete, for example, Gödel devised a system in which logical statements (that were very much like computer commands) could be rendered as numbers, dissolving the rigid distinction between syntax and data. Or, as von Neumann would put it in 1945 while describing the computer he was planning to build at the IAS: '"Words" coding the orders are handled in the memory just like numbers.' That is the essence of modern-day coding, the concept at the heart of software.

'Someone knowledgeable about modern programming languages today looking at Gödel's paper…will see a sequence of forty-five numbered formulas that looks very much like a computer program,' the mathematician Martin Davis explains. 'The resemblance is no accident. Gödel had to deal with many of the same issues that those designing programming languages and those writing programs in those languages would be facing.'

Turing's achievement, by contrast, was to describe in abstract terms imaginary machines that could read, write or erase symbols on an infinitely long tape. In his paper, 'On Computable Numbers, with an Application to the Entscheidungsproblem', Turing painstakingly builds a 'universal machine'. When fed the coded description of any other Turing machine, the universal machine can simulate it exactly.

The whole logical apparatus of Turing's paper was assembled to answer Hilbert's *Entscheidungsproblem*. With it, he proved there can be no general, systematic process for deciding whether or not any particular mathematical statement is provable, dashing the last of Hilbert's dreams. Though no one recognised it as such at the time, Turing's 'universal machine' is now considered an abstract prototype of a general purpose 'stored program' computer – one that can, like any laptop or smartphone today, execute any application in the computer's memory. The proofs of 'On Computable Numbers' arrived while Turing was in Princeton as a visiting fellow, a post he had secured in part because of a letter of recommendation from von Neumann. Turing was disappointed with his paper's reception there. But one person did take notice. 'Turing's office was right near von Neumann's, and von Neumann was very interested in that kind of thing,' says Goldstine. 'I'm sure that von Neumann understood the significance of Turing's work when the time came.'

With the EDVAC report, von Neumann turned Gödel's and Turing's abstract musings into the canonical blueprint for the stored-program computer. Because he did not wish to get bogged down in the specifics of engineering, and because the ENIAC was still classified as confidential, von Neumann described his computer in terms of idealised neurons, shorn of their physiological complexities, which came from work published by the neurophysiologist Warren McCulloch and the mathematician Walter Pitts in 1943. This seems odd today, but von Neumann, Turing, Norbert Wiener and other thinkers who contributed to the foundations of the field that became known as artificial intelligence did think about computers as electronic brains. Today, using 'brain' or 'neuron' in the context of computers seems laughably naive. Yet we accept the similarly anthropomorphic use of 'memory' to mean 'storage' without blinking an eye.

McCulloch-Pitts neurons are vastly simplified electronic versions of a neuron. In his EDVAC report, von Neumann wires networks of these 'neurons' together to make five components or 'organs', each with a different function. The first three components he described were a 'central arithmetic' unit for performing mathematical operations, such as addition and multiplication; a 'central control' unit to ensure that instructions were executed in the proper order; and a 'memory', a single organ that would store both computer code and numbers. The fourth and fifth components were the input and output units, for shipping data into or out of the machine.

Computer designers now refer to the whole configuration as the 'von Neumann architecture', and nearly all computers in use today – smartphones, laptops, desktops – are built according to its precepts. The design's fundamental drawback, now called the 'von Neumann bottleneck', is that instructions or data have to be found and fetched serially from memory, like standing in a line and being able to pass messages only forwards or backwards. That task takes much longer than any subsequent processing. That handicap is outweighed by the architecture's considerable advantages, which stem from its simplicity. The ENIAC had 20 modules that could add and subtract, for example; in the EDVAC, there would be one. Less circuitry means less that can go wrong, and a more reliable machine. Historian Thomas Haigh and colleagues describe the aesthetics of von Neumann's report as 'radical minimalism, akin to high modernist architecture or design'. 'His intellectual response to ENIAC,' they say in their book, ENIAC *in Action*, 'might be likened to that of a Calvinist zealot who, having taken charge of a gaudy cathedral, goes to work whitewashing frescos and lopping off ornamental flourishes.'

When Goldstine received the report, he was in raptures. He congratulated von Neumann for providing the first 'complete logical framework for the machine' and contrasted the streamlined design with the ENIAC, which was 'chuck full of gadgets that have as their only raison d'être that they appealed to John Mauchly'. He had the report typed up, and sent out dozens of copies to nascent computer groups all over the world.

Not everyone was pleased. The report Goldstine circulated only had the name John von Neumann on its title page. Eckert and Mauchly, who were hoping to patent aspects of computer design, were furious. The ENIAC's inventors accused von Neumann of inflating his contribution to the project and rehashing their work.

Von Neumann, for his part, feared that the commercial route the ENIAC's inventors were pursuing would stifle progress. The purpose of the EDVAC report, von Neumann testified in 1947, was 'to contribute to clarifying and coordinating the thinking of the group' and 'further…the art of building high speed computers' by disseminating the work as quickly and as widely as possible. 'My personal opinion was at all times, and is now, that this was perfectly proper and in the best interests of the United States,' he observed.

'I certainly intend to do my part to keep as much of this field "in the public domain" (from the patent point of view) as I can,' von Neumann wrote as he made plans for building his own computer at the IAS. Patent rights to the IAS machine were in large part handed over to the government in mid-1947. Von Neumann and Goldstine sent a stream of detailed progress reports to about 175 institutions in several different countries, spawning the first generation of modern computers across the world.

Britain's Small-Scale Experimental Machine, nicknamed the 'Manchester Baby', sputtered into life in 1948. Often said to be the world's first electronic stored-program computer, the Baby was based on the EDVAC design and on 21 June that year cycled through 17 commands over 52 minutes to determine that the highest factor of 262,144 is 131,072. But weeks earlier, von Neumann's second wife, Klára Dán, had helped to rewire the ENIAC into a sort of EDVAC-style computer. Klára, who describes herself as a 'mathematical moron' in her memoirs, would also write the first code to run on the ENIAC in its new configuration. Her 800-command program, simulating the paths of neutrons inside an atom bomb, was the first truly useful, complex modern program ever to have been executed on a computer.

Von Neumann's own computer at the IAS finally began work in 1951. By this time, the IAS machine's numerous offspring, built with the aid of von Neumann and Goldstine's numerous detailed updates, were snapping at its heels. Perhaps most important among them was the IBM 701, the company's first commercial computer and practically a carbon copy of the one built at the IAS. By the 1960s, IBM manufactured about 70% of the world's electronic computers. 'Probably, the IBM company owes half its money to Johnny von Neumann,' von Neumann's friend, the Hungarian physicist Edward Teller, would tell his biographers.

In 1965, Intel's co-founder, Gordon Moore, predicted that the number of components on an integrated circuit would double every year. His observation became known as 'Moore's law', but von Neumann had beaten him to it a decade earlier, by noting that the overall capacity of computers had nearly doubled every year since 1945 and implying, in conversation, that he expected that trend to continue.

The battle for ownership of the intellectual property and patent rights relating to the ENIAC and EDVAC would drag on for decades. Long after von Neumann's death in 1957, the judge's verdict, delivered on 19 October 1973, held the automatic electronic digital computer to be in the public domain. The open source movement, born a decade or so later, would soon shun corporate secrecy, lauding the benefits of freely sharing information to drive forward innovation. But thanks to von Neumann, those principles were baked into computing from the very beginning.

Babbage designed the 'Analytical Engine', a mechanical general purpose computer that was never built. Lovelace wrote a program for it that never ran and her work was rediscovered only long after the first EDVAC-style stored-program computers were built. Turing would cite the EDVAC report nine months after its publication, as he made his own plans for a computer, the Automatic Computing Engine (ACE), and his theoretical work was retrospectively appropriated as a foundation stone of computer science. Yet the names of John von Neumann and Klára Dán, innovators who helped birth the computer age, have faded inexplicably from view.

*The Burning of the Houses of Lords
and Commons, 16 October 1834,*
Joseph Mallord William Turner, 1835.

THE EIGHTEENTH-CENTURY TECHNOLOGICAL AWAKENING OF ARTIST ADVENTURERS

Andrew Wilton

When the Royal Academy of Arts was founded in London under the patronage of King George III in 1768, the painters, sculptors and architects who made up the pioneering group had to decide on a suitable president to represent them on the public stage. The obvious candidate was the portrait painter Joshua Reynolds: accomplished, highly successful, and with a wide circle of eminent and learned friends.

Reynolds represented and advocated the academic principle of respect for the Old Masters of Italy, Spain and the Netherlands and a preference for serious literary and historical subjects. (He considered his own speciality, portraiture, second best.) He set out this high-minded programme in his *Discourses* to the students, but in his own earnest efforts at history painting he almost always failed.

It was part of his pre-eminence that he took a creative interest in the actual techniques of painting. Striving after grand effects, he was always experimenting with new materials, and his most ambitious canvases are now illegible ghosts because of his inventive adoption of substances such as bitumen and wax, which he mixed with his pigments to enhance their depth and glow. Go to Petworth House in Sussex, and see one of the biggest of them, *Macbeth and the Witches*. It covers a large wall, and is an almost indecipherable, darkened wreck, a monument to his laudable curiosity.

He was far from being the only experimenter. There is a picture in the Tate by a history painter of the next generation, William Hilton. It is a night scene, a dramatic historical subject: *Editha and the Monks Searching for the Body of Harold*, and it measures an appropriately enormous 334× 243 centimetres. Hilton showed it at the Academy in 1834. But it cannot be exhibited now. It is the sad remains of an experiment similar to Reynolds's *Macbeth*: the semi-liquid bitumen with which it was painted – the 'mummy' in which the ancient Egyptians embalmed their dead –

has never dried, and the canvas has to be turned like a mattress every few years so the pigment can flow back to its proper place.

The spirit of invention and exploration among the Academicians is wonderfully spoofed in the great satirist James Gillray's print *Titianus Redivivus* (Titian Reborn), published in 1797. It shows several leading artists taken in by a spurious 'Venetian Secret', concocted and promoted by a young woman, Mary Anne Provis, and her father. Several of them had paid ten guineas apiece for this quack recipe. Others, including the 22-year-old J. M. W. Turner, are not fooled. Reynolds, who had died in 1792, is present as an appalled spirit, but one cannot help wondering if he might have been attracted to the claim that the methods of one of the greatest painters of the Italian Renaissance had been revealed to Miss Provis, and been tempted to try it, simply for the sake of experimenting.

A student at the Academy Schools was the young William Blake. He came to despise the institution and wrote scurrilously about Reynolds as a traitor to the art he practised. He never became a member, but he followed Reynolds's lead in trying out materials that proved disastrous for his pictures. He invented a medium that he called 'fresco', a version of *tempera*, not much related to the system the Renaissance Italians had used to cover their walls and ceilings. The elaborate subject-pictures that he painted using it – *The Spiritual Form of Pitt Guiding Behemoth* and *The Spiritual Form of Nelson Guiding Leviathan,* among others – have deteriorated just as much as Reynolds's much larger works, to become cracked and blackened wrecks. But he had more success with a highly idiosyncratic version of the medium of etching, for the purpose of printing his own *Prophetic Books* of visionary poetry, which he (or his wife Catherine) would colour by hand and issue in tiny editions for the few people interested in his now much-prized arcana.

The fact is that the Royal Academy, like its products, like the country as a whole, was a technological melting pot. It was the youngest of the artists' academies established in Europe over the past 200 years to embody and promote their professional aspirations and status. They had all laid down standards that ensured the quality of work remained high. In London, the same objectives held good, and it was clearly understood among the artists that their aims were more refined, more exclusively aesthetic, than the mere mechanical crafts. But London was not Rome, Copenhagen or Paris. It was the capital city of a country caught up in the civilisation-altering toils of the first Industrial Revolution. Only a few years earlier, a Society for the Encouragement of Arts, Manufactures and Commerce had been founded in London, awarding premiums for works of scientific invention and ingenuity as well as for essays in design and draughtsmanship. It was a leading institution of the Age of the Enlightenment. In the year of the Academy's first exhibition, 1769, Thomas Arkwright unveiled his spinning machine which was to help revolutionise the manufacture of cloth. Earlier in the decade, in 1763, James Hargreaves's spinning jenny had started the process. In between, in 1765, James Watt had invented his condenser, which ten years later was to produce the first steam engine.

Also in 1769, Josiah Wedgwood opened his Etruria pottery works in Burslem, Staffordshire, an initiative that married technology with art and design in ways that survive today. A very early academician straddling the two disciplines was George Stubbs, the renowned painter of horses, who executed pictures in enamel, a very unconventional medium, on thin ceramic panels that Wedgwood produced specially for him. Stubbs exhibited the resulting paintings at the Royal Academy in 1782, where they caused a furore. And his attitude to his art was scientific; he brought a dead horse into his Lincolnshire barn and dissected it over many weeks, making careful drawings of the anatomy. These he published for their informative value in their own right.

Much of the impetus for the technological revolution of the age came from the newly expanding cities of the Midlands, with their coal and steel industries, where groups of businessmen, industrialists and scientists met to exchange ideas about science and technology. The Lunar Society is the best known of these groups. It came into existence in the mid-1760s, and Josiah Wedgwood was one of its early members, as were Thomas Arkwright, the chemist Joseph Priestley, the industrialist Matthew Boulton, and Erasmus Darwin, Charles Darwin's grandfather. Closely associated with several of these was the Derby painter Joseph Wright, who was elected an Associate of the Royal Academy in 1781. Shortly after, he celebrated the cotton mills that Arkwright had built a decade earlier in a view of them by the light of a serene full moon. The unromantic, eminently functional factory buildings are presented as the focus of an atmospheric night scene.

Moonlight, firelight, candlelight: Wright painted all these effects in a spirit of investigation, of scientific research, even while making the most of their value as visual poetry. This double intention lies behind his famous depictions of an orrery – a model of the solar system – and *An Experiment with the Air-pump*, both seen by candlelight, with all the expressive human nuances of fascinated faces seen in *chiaroscuro*. In the *Air-pump*, the scientist – or is he a magician? – working the contraption, a seventeenth-century invention, is about to turn off the supply of air to a white bird in a bell-like glass receiver. A scientist takes notes, an old man ponders the idea of death, children try not to watch, lovers take advantage of the darkness to canoodle. It's a disquisition on human nature in relation to the achievements of science. This and *The Orrery* are among the greatest and most original paintings of the age.

An art form that developed astonishingly in this period was landscape. It lent itself particularly to experiments with media and methods. One of its greatest exponents, the Suffolk-born Thomas Gainsborough, forged his career by painting portraits but, like Reynolds, always wanted to do something else. In his case, it was landscape he experimented with, not only painting specific places but inventing compositions that obeyed rules of harmony, proportion and balance as true abstractions. For these explorations he sometimes painted on glass, so that the luminous sky could be presented with real light by holding the pane up to a candle. The theory of abstract design in painting had been laid out and published by an art master at Eton, Alexander Cozens, whose son, John Robert, reversed the process and applied it to real places, such as scenes in the Alps or the Italian Campagna.

It was inevitable that the theatrical possibilities of light and landscape should break out from their confinement on canvas or paper and become three-dimensional experiences. Philippe-Jacques de Loutherbourg, a painter from Alsace who became a full academician in 1781, created a theatre stage ten feet by six feet wide that he called *the Eidophusikon*, in which he showed scenes that were not stationary but presented altering phenomena: Aurora, or the Effects of Dawn; Tangiers at noon; Naples with a sunset; or a view of London from Greenwich Park. There was a storm at sea with thunder and lightning, using a battery of equipment including moving scenery, coloured slides and mirrors, as well as musical accompaniment. These dramatic scenes chimed with the current fashion for 'the Sublime', a notion considered important and much discussed in contexts both philosophical and aesthetic.

Other artists enlarged the technical range of picture-making along similar lines by developing the Panorama – a complete 360-degree circular painting that you stood or sat in the centre of and could imagine yourself present at an actual event, whether the meeting of all the devils in the Pandemonium of Milton's *Paradise Lost*, or a tranquil morning on the roof of a tall London building. Several academicians contributed sensational, enormous paintings to the repertoire, notably 'mad' John Martin, whose vision of *Belshazzar's Feast* was a typical specimen of his heightened vision. The word 'panorama' was invented (or stolen from the Greek) in 1791, and as a form of popular entertainment and instruction it spread throughout Europe and America and begat even more elaborate devices that were the forerunners of cinema.

Many artists experimented with transparencies – either on glass, or sheets of paper painted to be partly opaque, so that when a candle was placed behind them an illuminated scene appeared; a cottage by moonlight, for instance. As a young man, Turner tried his hand at a few of these. Another landscape painter who used sheets of glass for his studies was John Constable, who emphasised that he saw his own art as part of the scientific endeavour of the age. He thought of his pictures, small or large, as scientific experiments, not only his rapid notes of meteorological effects but even the full-size sketches for his six-footers, which he kept simply as trials for the finished works he would send for exhibition at the Academy. The comparison between the sketches and the finished pictures reveals how much his experiments taught him, with the final version embodying much of the impromptu technique and vibrancy of the sketch. This was the dawn of a totally fresh approach to painting, a new union of technique and emotion, parallel, we might say, to the experiments in verse that Wordsworth and Coleridge made in their *Lyrical Ballads* of 1798. 'Painting is but another word for feeling,' observed Constable – a truly modern idea! It is no coincidence that he was popular in France, where his *Hay Wain* won a medal at the Paris Salon in 1824. Impressionism was not far down the historical line, but Constable had already got there.

He distanced himself from the academicians who took a long time electing him one of their number, and did so only grudgingly in the end. He laughed at what he called the 'high-minded' members 'who stickle for the "elevated & noble" walks of art – i.e. preferring the shaggy posteriors of a Satyr to the moral feeling of a landscape'. By comparison, Turner (a year older) thought of himself as continuing the great European tradition, treating landscape as grandly as if it were history painting.

But in a quite different way he, too, was technically extremely adventurous. By the age of 25 Turner had developed watercolour into a new medium, capable of much the same expressive power as oils, and he used it to paint grand historical subjects too. The large watercolour views he made in North Wales in 1798 are among the great landscapes of European art. He would have been a major master if he had died in 1800. But he lived another half-century, constantly expanding the technical range of his work.

He kept his methods to himself and people were correspondingly keen to find out how he did it, whether in oil or in watercolour. He was seen as a wizard in both media, and there are excited reports from lucky witnesses of his procedures. A boy who was allowed to watch him painting a watercolour of a huge battleship (from memory) told his family: 'He began by pouring wet paint until it was saturated, he tore, he scratched, he scrubbed at it in a kind of frenzy and the whole thing was chaos – but gradually and as if by magic the lovely ship, with all its exquisite minutia, came into being...'

Much later in his life he took to performing these kinds of transformation scenes in public, or at least in front of his fellow academicians, who crowded around (while pretending not to look), on the 'varnishing days' before the annual exhibition opened, rather like the audience gathered around Wright of Derby's scientist (or conjuror?) with his air pump, or the visitors to De Loutherbourg's *Eidophusikon*. In 1835, Turner submitted one of his two spectacular treatments of *The Burning of the Houses of Lords and Commons*, and a fellow academician reported: '...the picture when sent in was a mere dab of several colours, and without form and void, like chaos before the creation...since he began in the morning – he never ceased to work, or even once looked or turned from the wall on which his picture hung...A small box of colours, a very few small brushes, and a vial or two, were at his feet, very inconveniently placed... In one part of the mysterious proceedings Turner, who worked almost entirely with his palette knife, was observed to be rolling and spreading a lump of half-transparent stuff over his picture, the size of a finger in length and thickness...presently the work was finished: Turner gathered up his tools together, put them into and shut up the box, and then, with his face still turned to the wall, and at the same distance from it, went sideling [*sic*] off, without speaking a word to anybody...All looked with a half-wondering smile, and Maclise, who stood near, remarked, "There, that's masterly, he does not stop to look at his work; he *knows* it is done, and he is off."'

Turner transformed his own paintings into performance art but, as we have seen, that was exactly in the spirit of the times.

Interior of RAF Fylingdales radomes,
North York Moors, England, 1994.

REWIRING THE WORLD

Brendan Simms and Constance Simms

It is often suggested that the technology revolution has transformed international politics. There is no doubt that technology has changed our daily lives at a speed inconceivable even two decades ago. Today, a toddler who can navigate a smartphone has access to more information than Ronald Reagan did as president of the United States.

But has tech really, as some argue, transcended traditional geopolitics? Are the new battle lines no longer traditional ones between nation states but those created by transnational competition between coalitions of 'netizens' across state boundaries? Is it the case, as Niall Ferguson eloquently argued in his *The Square and the Tower*, that these new networks are rewiring international relations? To answer these questions we must first consider what the historical connection between technological change and geopolitical shifts has been.

In 1430, Europe had not seen a major technical innovation since the Romans. The exception was gunpowder, developed in China for medicinal purposes before its use in warfare became widespread towards the end of the Middle Ages. It transformed the battlefield and social relations. Knights became redundant, although the feudal order underpinning them proved remarkably resilient at first. What gunpowder did not do was change the geopolitical dynamic itself. The Ottoman Turks had a distinct edge in siege artillery, for example, but this would merely accelerate their advance, which had begun long before then. Gunpowder became simply another weapon in European conflicts of the time, such as the Anglo-French Hundred Years' War, and the perennial struggle for supremacy in the Holy Roman Empire.

Then Johannes Gutenberg wrought what Elizabeth Eisenstein famously christened, in the title of her book, *The Printing Revolution in Early Modern Europe*. To be sure, the invention of print facilitated literacy and fuelled the Reformation. But the effects were more cultural than geopolitical. The largest single issue addressed in books printed in the first 80 years or so after Gutenberg typeset his first text was the Turkish threat, and the related political fragmentation of Christendom, not its theological divisions. Printing did not fundamentally affect the key power struggles of the time, such as that between the Habsburg and Valois dynasties in Italy and Germany.

Likewise, if we review the European state system at the start of the nineteenth century, the continuities are as evident as the changes. The seventeenth and eighteenth centuries saw enormous strides in shipbuilding and navigation, including the invention of copper-bottomed hulls which enabled ships to stay at sea for longer; and the discovery of 'longitude' facilitated navigation. Taken together, maritime innovation and artillery gave Europeans the edge over Asian actors, at least so long as they stuck to the high seas and coastal areas, and a devastating advantage over African and Indigenous American polities.

That said, it was not any technological imbalance that led to the French defeat during the Revolutionary and Napoleonic wars, but the disparity in resources. So little had changed in some of Europe's fundamental geopolitical alignments that the great confrontation between France and what was to become Great Britain between 1689 and 1815 became known as the 'Second Hundred Years' War'. The Holy Roman Empire, soon to become the German Confederation, remained a site of furious contestation. Of course, some powers like Spain had receded in importance, while Russia and Prussia had emerged. In both of these cases, however, success was the product not of technological innovation but of size and organisation.

As one observer has pointed out, Napoleon had crossed the Alps pretty much as Hannibal had, on the back of an animal. In the mid-nineteenth century, however, travel was about to be revolutionised. Steam power liberated passengers and cargo from the trade winds. The advent of railways drove huge social and economic change in the nineteenth and early twentieth centuries. Regions were integrated more closely, and economies were no longer bound by inland waterways. Labour mobility was greatly facilitated.

This led to a new phase in the relationship between technology and geopolitics. For example, the weakness of the tsarist rail network meant that in the mid-1850s the faraway British and French could reinforce their armies in the Crimea by sea, more quickly than the much closer Russians could do by land. Prussia's victory over Austria in 1866 also owed a lot to her superior rail system (and weaponry). Later, people would speak of 1914 as a 'war by railway timetable'.

All the same, the connection between technological shifts and geo-political ones was not straightforward. First, some developments – like railways and steamships – cancelled each other out or were perceived to do so. In the late nineteenth and early twentieth century, for example, students of geopolitics were divided between followers of the American naval theorist Alfred Thayer Mahan, who believed that sea power was the key to success, and those of the British geographer Sir Halford Mackinder, who held that the advent of rail gave the 'heartland' powers of Eurasia the edge, because they could operate on interior lines.

Secondly, technological progress tended to be shared quite quickly, for example when Britain's *dreadnought* battleships were speedily copied by other powers in the early twentieth century; or when aircraft, though invented in the United States, were adopted as weapons platforms by all the main belligerents. There were many encounters in Africa when better-armed Europeans mowed down their African or Arab enemies, such as the slaughter of the Mahdists by the British at Omdurman, Sudan in 1898, but there were few major and sustained technological imbalances in the contests between European powers.

Many thought the invention of flight, the most dramatic scientific leap of the early twentieth century, would fundamentally transform geopoli-tics. Observing the experimental flights of the Brazilian aviation pioneer Alberto Santos-Dumont in November 1906, the press baron Lord Northcliffe remarked, 'England is no longer an island. It means the aerial chariots of a foe descending on British soil if war comes.' His organ, the *Daily Mail*, wrote of 'the military problem caused by the virtual annihila-tion of frontiers and the acquisition of the power to pass readily through the air above the sea'. This meant, the newspaper predicted, that 'the iso-lation of the United Kingdom may disappear.' Not long after, the British government began to support the development of military aviation, which soon became a major arm of industry.

The effect of all this was not to render old strategic paradigms redun-dant, but to reinforce them. The principal bases for any aerial attack on England would likely be in the historical areas of concern: northern France and the Low Countries. Indeed, time was to show that the aero-plane, far from being simply a danger to the country, could also serve for its defence, and as a sally port into continental Europe.

Of course, during the first half of the last century scientific advances affected battlefield outcomes significantly. Two instances are radar and the ASDIC sonar system, with respect to the war at sea and in the air. That said, technology did not cause or decide either conflict. The US–Japanese rivalry, which nearly resulted in war in 1905, emerged some time before aircraft were invented, and long before the invention of the aircraft carrier. Japan was defeated not because American planes and ships were better, though that was increasingly the case, but because the United States could build many more of them; it would have prevailed even without the atom bomb. Likewise, the key disparity between the German Reich and its antagonists in both world wars was not technological but their vastly different demographic and industrial capacities. Quantity, not quality or innovation, was the decisive factor.

This subordinate relationship between technology and geopolitics holds true even for the Cold War, sometimes dubbed 'The Nuclear Age'. Clearly, the advent of weapons of mass destruction at Hiroshima and Nagasaki changed the nature of warfare. It is less obvious, though, that they affected deeper geopolitical patterns. The antagonism between communist dictatorship and Western democracy predated nuclear power, and the brief American monopoly did not much constrain Stalin. He merely noted that the protagonists needed 'strong nerves' as a result. Nor did the move into space, a whole new dimension, change the fundamental dynamic. It simply became another area of contestation between the superpowers.

The two final decades of the Cold War saw the start of the 'information revolution' in the West with the invention of the microchip. The inability of Moscow to keep up with technology epitomised the failure of communism, but it did not bring down the Wall or shatter the Soviet Union. That was primarily the work of other forces. Internally, the East proved unable to cope with the forces set free by Gorbachev's policies, and externally, Moscow had been worn down by failure in Afghanistan and other theatres. The effects of the microchip-driven 'revolution in military affairs', which made the United States a peerless competitor on land, at sea and in the air throughout the 1990s, were not visible until the wars in Iraq and the former Yugoslavia. It was only then that one saw a 'unipolar moment' when Western, and particularly US dominance, was underpinned by a 'full spectrum dominance' across all platforms.

This development coincided with the next stage of the information revolution, the growth of the internet – itself an outgrowth of the US defence complex – and then of social media like Facebook, Twitter, Instagram and Snapchat. These transformations, and the accompanying surge in economic interdependence through globalisation, caused many to bid goodbye not merely to the nation state but to classic interstate competition altogether.

Some argue that social media, unlike other new technologies, is much more than a tool. The recent, and much-discussed, Netflix documentary *The Social Dilemma* suggests that the continuing tech revolution is not just the latest frontier but a completely new (and sinister) phenomenon. Boundaries today, the argument runs, are more fluid, and run within, rather than between, societies. Data, not territory, is the key battleground. Although there is something in this argument, there is not yet enough evidence to suggest that the traditional model of geopolitics is now redundant, or that social media will not prove to be ultimately subordinate to pre-existing geopolitical structures.

What is true is that social media, unlike any other tool, moulds itself to the user. It is personalised and addictive. It encourages polarisation by feeding existing prejudices and creating echo chambers which are hard to escape. Four years ago, Facebook's own analysts noted that its algorithms directed users towards extremist groups. 'Our recommendation system,' they admitted, 'grows the problem.' This is certainly part of the explanation for Donald Trump's election victory in 2016 and (to a much lesser degree) the outcome of the EU referendum in the UK earlier that year. In 2018, James Bridle addressed the resulting proliferation of 'fake news', conspiracy theories and fundamentalism in his book *New Dark Age: Technology and the End of the Future.* The events at the US Capitol in early 2021 showed the power of such mobilisation, and the subsequent banning of a sitting US president from various social media platforms raised even more profound questions.

But regardless of its impact on the domestic political sphere, social media has not transcended great power rivalries. Rather, it has been subsumed into them. The fundamental divide in the world today is not between various domestic tribes, or even transnational coalitions of such groups organising through social media, but between the West and its two main challengers, Russia and the People's Republic of China. The theatres of contention have been traditional: Putin's annexation of the Crimea, Sino-American jostling in the South China Sea and Taiwan

Straits, and Sino-Indian scuffles in Ladakh. The main battle over data has concerned the Chinese corporation Huawei. States matter more than ever, and bigger ones matter as much as before. So far, social media has proved to be simply another platform in a global struggle which would be taking place in any case.

In short, technological change affects international politics in both war and peace, but does not transform the system itself. The exception is the relationship between the West and the rest before the mid-twentieth century. The whole structure of Western imperialism in America, Africa and Asia rested on a technological imbalance, from Cortes's use of firearms against the Aztecs in the early sixteenth century to the deployment of poison gas by Mussolini against the Ethiopians in the 1930s. The atom bomb ended the war much sooner than it would otherwise have done, but Japan's defeat was still inevitable. Wars between the great powers have tended to be decided by skill (the German defeat of France in 1940) or, more often, by attrition (as in the First and Second World Wars). Whoever comes out on top between China and the West, the outcome will ultimately be decided not by their respective technological strengths, important though those will be, but by their relative military, economic and societal resilience in times of severe stress.

There is a parallel here between the pattern of geopolitics and that of domestic transformation, at least in Britain. The sociologist W. G. Runciman titled his celebrated investigation of British society over the past 300 years *Very Different, But Much The Same: The Evolution of English Society Since 1714* (2013). He did not mean to suggest little had changed between 1714 and the present day; clearly many things had, and very profoundly. Rather, Runciman had in mind the continuity of institutions and societal traditions, for example intergenerational mobility, which made the Britain of the past recognisable to us today (and would have made us intelligible to them). In the same way, there is a fundamental geopolitical pattern over time, within which technological change operates, rather than the other way around. In this sense, the international systems traversed in this essay may be different, certainly with regard to their scientific make-up, but they are also geopolitically much the same.

Compare for example the alignments of today with those of the early Cold War. The Taiwan Straits crises of 1954–5 and 1958 look very familiar. So does the spectre of Kremlin-sponsored aggression in Europe. In 1962, India and China fought a brief but bloody war in almost exactly the same area that the two powers tussled over last year. As for disinformation and paranoia, the historian Calder Walton has recently shown that these were standard features of the time, since forgotten about. Finally, the idea that an outside power might capture the US presidency (a standard feature of the 'collusion with Russia' allegations made against Donald Trump) was dramatised more than 50 years earlier in the 1962 film *The Manchurian Candidate*. There is little new under the sun.

Of course, just because technology has not decisively shaped geopolitics in the past doesn't mean it never will. Artificial intelligence, today shorthand for machine learning, may well prove to be the game changer of cliché. AI could develop a mind of its own and bring about the war of computers that was so narrowly averted in the 1983 film *WarGames*. We cannot be sure that tech will not transform geopolitics, in the ways that its boosters celebrate and its detractors fear. We just haven't seen much evidence of it yet.

Gas oil installation on the coast of Qatar.

THE GEOPOLITICAL FIGHT TO COME OVER
GREEN ENERGY

Helen Thompson

The world is cornered in a Janus-faced energy crisis: one generated by the speed with which it is necessary to replace fossil fuel energy to stop global temperatures rising, and one around oil, on which, even in three decades' time, even if carbon neutrality is achieved, the world economy and everyday life will still depend. For all the hope often expressed that the acute problems facing the oil sector are a vindication of the seismic shift in green ambitions over the past couple of years, there is in reality no escape from either side of this predicament.

An oil crisis was first evident in the middle years of the 2000s, when stagnant supply and sharply escalating Chinese demand sent oil prices soaring to an eventual peak, in real terms a third higher than their previous apex during the early part of the Iran–Iraq War. Since early in the last decade, the shale oil boom has prevented a repeat price shock. But it will prove a temporary lull on the supply side. A report published in 2017 by the banking giant HSBC suggested that more than 80% of existing conventional liquids production – non-shale and tar sands oil – is in decline. Once Saudi Arabia reacted to shale's ascent by inducing a price slump in late 2014, oil companies severely cut their investments. In 2019, oil production fell for the first time in a decade, even as consumption rose by almost one million barrels per day. Now, having stood for nearly a decade between the world economy and energy-driven recessions, the shale oil industry is in some trouble, savaged by the pandemic shock to demand, low investment and high debt costs.

Meanwhile, the climate crisis has escalated. Extreme weather events are increasing in number; in summer 2020, floods deluged much of east and south Asia; and this winter's disruption to the polar vortex left Texas freezing. Politically, climate has moved centre stage. Inspired by Greta Thunberg's school strike, a mass climate movement emerged on the world's streets. In April 2019, Emmanuel Macron established a Citizens' Climate Convention, made up of 150 randomly chosen civilians and experts, asked to ascertain ways France could cut carbon emissions. Two months later, Britain became the first large state to legislate for a legally binding net zero emissions target. By the end of that year, the EU too had committed to carbon neutrality by 2050 and declared its intention to decouple economic growth from resource use. Last September, Xi Jinping announced to the United Nations that China aimed to achieve net zero by 2060.

Changes in capital flows tie prospects for oil supply and the recent political momentum together. Investment in ESG (environmental, social and corporate governance) has seen many large pension funds commit to achieving carbon-neutral portfolios by 2050. Against this backdrop, share prices of American and European oil companies fell in 2019 and crashed in 2020. The big European oil companies are trying to reinvent themselves: BP, Total and Shell all have carbon-neutral aims, and the Italian multinational Eni has said it will reduce emissions by 80% by 2050. By contrast, American companies have been more reluctant to change, and look in even more immediate difficulty. The market cap of ExxonMobil, the single biggest heir to Standard Oil, is now around 300% lower than its peak in 2007. In August 2020, the company lost its near-century-long membership of the Dow Jones Industrial Average. After activist investor groups targeted the company by trying to gain seats on the board, Exxon scrambled to push a five-year emissions reduction plan.

But if the drive to invest large sums to decarbonise reflects the change in political consciousness around climate, moving away from fossil fuels remains a Herculean task. When the first UN Climate Change Conference was held in Berlin in 1995, fossil fuels constituted 86% of the world's primary energy consumption. By 2019, that proportion had fallen by just 2%. In 2018, the increase in fossil fuel production was more than three times higher than the increase in renewables. The following year, the annual increase in fossil fuel energy consumption was slightly under that of renewables. The primary difference was that 2019 had the slowest growth in the world economy for a decade.

The 'energy transition' tag is a misnomer. Radically reducing fossil fuel energy will represent an energy and an economic revolution. The difficulty is not a matter of political will or money, but physics. As the Czech-Canadian environmental scientist Vaclav Smil – the one energy realist that techno-optimist Bill Gates takes absolutely seriously – has repeatedly pointed out, a green energy revolution would be qualitatively different than any energy change in human history because it involves moving from more concentrated to less concentrated energy, rather than in the opposite direction.

However much companies and governments promise dramatic and rapid change, their deeds and small-print rhetoric point to the hard consequences of this reality. BP may be heralding a low carbon energy future, but its own 2020 annual report presumes the world will still be using between 80 and 100 million barrels of oil a day in 2040. The same report says that 'significant levels of investment are required for there to be sufficient supplies of oil to meet demand in 2040.' It takes some cognitive dissonance to believe this oil could still be produced whilst investors shut capital out of the privately owned oil industry; that is, unless it is accepted that all future oil comes from Russia's Rosneft and the Middle Eastern state-owned oil companies and is so expensive as to act as an impediment to growth. Still owning 19.75% of Rosneft, BP has clearly hedged how it thinks the energy future will play out.

Decarbonising the electricity sector is easier than replacing oil in transportation and petrochemicals, but, as with fossil fuels, geography ensures that not all states are equal in the options available. Germany began its *Energiewende* early. But Germany has among the highest electricity prices in the world. In a speech in January 2020, Angela Merkel admitted 'it is unlikely that it will be possible to achieve a 100% share of renewable energies in electricity generation…because the efficiency with which we can generate electricity from the wind and sun isn't very high. There are regions in the world where this works much better.'

Securing political consent to any changes that necessarily lower economic activity or threaten existing lifestyles is its own further Herculean task. The EU only agreed its European Green Deal in December 2019 by giving coal-heavy Poland an opt-out. In June 2020, Macron said he accepted all but one of the proposals generated by the Citizens' Climate Convention, only to water them down when presenting them to parliament. Fearful of the voters who were not represented at a convention dominated by those passionate about the green cause, and with spare time to pursue it, he protested: 'You can't say that because 150 citizens wrote something, it's the Bible or the Koran! I'm really very angry at those activists who helped me at first but are now saying – "you need to adopt it all."'

The geopolitics is little better because it involves a reckoning with China's power. During Donald Trump's presidency, this problem was frequently brushed aside. Trump's repudiation of the 2015 Paris Accord turned climate politics into a symbol of abandoned multilateralism. But the Paris Accord was deeply unpopular among establishment Republicans too, and not just because many Republicans in Congress take donations from fossil fuel energy companies. For Republicans, the Paris Accord was a matter of China policy, since it allowed China's emissions to continue to rise until 2030 whilst America's were supposed to fall by more than a quarter by 2025. The agreement also did nothing to stop China financing coal power stations abroad as part of the Belt and Road initiative. In practice, China's own emissions did decline in 2016. But, in another illustration of the current relationship between fossil fuel energy and economic growth, 2016 was a troubled year for China's economy. When it recovered in 2017, emissions began rising again.

The American return to Paris cannot take climate out of the geopolitical realm. Less oil and gas means the United States giving up the partial energy independence it procured by shale. More renewables yield economic advantages to China, since it dominates in solar energy manufacturing and materials. They will also drive a frenzied competition in mineral mining and control over land where essential components of batteries like lithium and cobalt lie. If the Green New Deal is supposed to also act as an industrial strategy for America to compete with China in these areas, then the latter will likely intensify its commitment to the country's strategic plan and industrial policy programme, Made in China 2025.

In Europe, renewables may appear to be a chance for a geopolitical reset, an escape from the present world in which Europe is burdened by high external energy dependency and an entrance into one where European firms become world leaders. But thus far this ambition has meant the EU hugging China closer at a time when it is ending Hong Kong's autonomy and systematically suppressing the Uighurs. In Merkel's January 2020 speech, she described working with China on climate as a 'tremendous opportunity' and envisaged connecting Europe's carbon trading system to China's 'to serve as an example'. Her implicit point of contrast was the United States. Yet during the Trump years American emissions fell and China's sharply rose. Xi appears well aware of the strategic opening the European projections on climate politics give China. By conceding the Comprehensive Agreement on Investment to the EU at the end of 2020, just a few months after offering his commitment on carbon neutrality, Xi has made it likely that when green energy manufacturing becomes central to Sino-American trade conflicts, Germany and France will be disinclined to ally with Washington.

This emerging green geopolitics is entirely predictable. Energy has been central to geopolitics since the Industrial Revolution. Oil-fuelled American industrialisation induced frenzied fears in Europe. From the 1870s, the conjunction of American oil resources allied to a continental single market and a high-tariff customs union drove a European scramble for energy resources and land empires in Africa. After the discovery of oil in the Middle East at a time when the US was moving to an oil-based navy, Britain, France and Germany competed over the crumbling Ottoman empire. Britain's victory in that competition – helped by its ability to project land power from India into the Persian Gulf – left it with a Middle Eastern empire that was a pivotal feature of the Eurasian map until the late 1960s. Germany's defeat in the First World War was central to the Nazis' expansionist ambitions. From the mid-1920s, Hitler became obsessed with America's mass-produced automotive society and the domestic oil supply that fuelled it. In retaining Ford and General Motors' presence in Germany, Nazi industrial strategy used short-term technological dependency on the United States in order to bring American-level automated mass production to Germany. In Hitler's geopolitical fantasy, the autobahns which German producers had learned to build would stretch out across Eurasia under German control. During the Second World War, he conceived Operation Barbarossa as the German equivalent of the conquest of the American West, since Russia was where, on Europe's immediate borders, there were large quantities of oil.

If large-scale energy change invites disorder, the fact that this energy revolution constitutes a reversal in energy density will also have historically singular consequences. When, in 1908, Henry Ford transformed car production and car ownership with his Model T, Standard Oil was already using large quantities of gasoline in its own machinery. Although Ford's new cars could run on either oil or alcohol-based ethanol – and Ford himself later became an advocate for alcohol fuel – the rise of the Model T and the ascendancy of Standard Oil are part of the same story. Now, electric car manufacturers do not have a scalable energy source immediately available to replicate internal combustion engines. Nor can they yet solve the issue of battery longevity, since the electricity to charge batteries needs to come from non-carbon primary energy. This energy revolution is a medium to long-term bet on technology in a mass storage capacity that does not yet exist.

So far as large-scale electrification in transportation is achievable, it will almost certainly lead to reduced energy consumption. Merkel has observed that this attempted energy revolution 'means turning our backs on our entire way of doing business and our entire way of life'. In its 2019 'Clean Growth' report, the House of Commons Science and Technology Committee noted that 'in the long-term, widespread personal vehicle ownership does not appear to be compatible with significant decarbonisation.'

This scenario is likely to have profound political implications. Elon Musk may talk about Tesla's Model 3 being for the mass market, but Henry Ford could sincerely vow that he was 'democratising the automobile'. Indeed, the Model T was in part Ford's response to the risk of political disorder that the arrival of cars created. Two years before his factory began churning out vehicles, future American President Woodrow Wilson warned that 'Nothing has spread Socialistic feeling in this country more than the use of automobiles.' The first cars let loose a romantic idea of freedom for a few that most people could not enjoy. This is memorably captured in the story of Toad of Toad Hall. Published in the year of Model T, 1908, *The Wind in the Willows* portrays the arrival of an 'exceptionally powerful motor car' for the rich and aristocratic Toad as an agent of chaos around the riverbank, transforming its owner into 'an Object which throws any decent-minded animal that comes across it into a violent fit'. Now, the direction of travel may well be back to the kind of world the Model T began to end.

The economic and political narratives that dominate collective life in Europe and North America leave us ill-equipped to deal with the energy troubles ahead. Many professional economists do not take energy seriously as a fundamental economic problem, let alone a political one. Some climate activism is divorced from the energy conditions of human existence, its proponents unwilling to grant that the laws of physics apply to energy prospects as much as to the climate.

To think about the energy origins of Western prosperity opens up difficult truths about the place of European empire and the United States' Middle Eastern wars in the economic history of the twentieth and early twenty-first centuries. Part of climate idealism contains a desire to leave this unpalatability behind, replacing fossil fuel imperialism with climate justice. But after the Second World War, Western economic life depended on the oil that came out of the Persian Gulf, through the Suez Canal, and into pipelines running to the Mediterranean. The counterfactual that eliminates past wrongs takes a lot else with it, including that which most people in Western democracies have little inclination to forsake. Given that battery production presently relies on cobalt mining done in grim conditions in the Democratic Republic of Congo, sometimes with child labour, and much of the solar-grade polysilicon used in solar panels is produced in Xinjiang, green energy will bring less ethical relief than often supposed.

Our cognitive struggles with energy matters extend to our concepts of historical time. Both the dread of a coming apocalypse and a faith in endless human innovation and moral improvement appear hardwired into Western culture, first from Christianity, and then its secular offshoot, the Enlightenment. When confronted with collective existential questions, Western minds reach rather easily to millenarian fears and hopes. Christianity began, after all, with the expectation of an apocalypse and the imminent arrival of God's kingdom. Although the Roman Catholic Church made Latin Christianity worldly, and Augustine slammed down millenarianism as delusional, the original Christian spirit lingered, readily available as a lens to give moral meaning to past sins in times of social and economic crisis. The apparent ideational clarity of the apocalyptic moment now permeates radical climate activism, captured in Extinction Rebellion's name as well as the movement's performative, and at times itinerant, political style.

But the temptation to make energy a Manichean struggle either between good and evil or science and unreason is decidedly unhelpful. There are Enlightenment optimists who cannot entertain doubt that technology will, godlike, prevail in establishing a new energy paradigm, regardless of the relationship between their certainty and physics. There are moral optimists who trust that, as human beings move from using dead sunlight to living sunlight, collective life will be ethically regenerated. These cannot be the stakes. The choices are much harder than either belief allows: to ask what might have to be sacrificed in dealing with China to try to stop it building more coal power stations is to recognise that a greener politics will not transcend tragedy. The stakes are also not so monumental: at least for the time being, there can be no green energy without fossil-fuel inputs is not going to end the world or human life.

Western democracies need practical strategies to accelerate techno-logical innovation in renewables, batteries and carbon capture as well as to address the coming problems around the supply of oil. They also need political strategies to contain the distributional consequences of reduced long-term energy consumption. The fact that what is necessary pulls in opposite directions is one of the great burdens of our times; it cannot be simplified to what our material aspirations and political imaginations can bear.

Scenes from a counting house, Cibo,
monk of Hyères, late fourteenth century.

THE ECONOMY AND THE PARADOX OF TECHNOLOGY

Samuel Gregg

'Ifthe heavens proclaim the glory of God, machines proclaim the glory of man,' wrote the Jesuit theologian and later cardinal Jean Daniélou in his 1961 book, *Scandaleuse vérité* (The Scandal of Truth). Technology, Daniélou understood, was in many ways a definitive feature of modernity, and represented the sharp end of humanity's ambition to master the world. In the early seventeenth century, Francis Bacon had described the scientific method's application to the natural world in his *Novum Organum Scientiarum* (1620) as restoring humans' 'rights over nature' as they use all their 'efforts to make the course of art outstrip nature'. In these words, we find much of the inspiration for the modern technological project.

Technology is a manifestation of empirical reason, and one sphere of life in which the application of empirical reason to our world has especially affected humans is the economy. The publication of Adam Smith's *Wealth of Nations* in 1776 launched the revolution of ideas that helped radically transform Western economic life, starting in Britain and then extending in rapid succession to continental Europe and the Americas. But while concepts like the division of labour and the mutually beneficial effects of free exchange proved critical in delivering millions of people from poverty, equally important was the emergence of devices such as the steam engine, pioneered by the English inventor Thomas Newcomen and enhanced by the Scottish engineer James Watt. What the Greeks called *tékhnē* – the knowledge of making and doing things – was as important as the new social science of economics.

The acceleration of technological change from the late eighteenth century onwards enabled humans to transform increasing amounts of raw materials into energy, to use that energy to create new tools and products out of combinations of other materials, and then trade these goods faster and more efficiently across the world. Since then, every successive generation has built upon their predecessors' technological achievements, to the point whereby people in developed economies today can order goods and services from across the world to their front door with a few clicks on their computer.

The pervasiveness of sophisticated technology is thus one of the defining features of modern economic life. But it has also had considerable spill-over effects that go beyond the economy. Some of these are especially evident in two sectors of Western economies: manufacturing and finance.

In many ways, the rise of modern capitalism was defined by manufacturing. The economist and historian of economic thought Joseph Schumpeter did not exaggerate when he wrote in his *History of Economic Analysis* (1954) that 'by the end of the fifteenth century most of the phenomena that we are in the habit of associating with that vague word "Capitalism" had put in their appearance, including big business, stock and commodity speculation, and "high finance"'. Technological change, however, was slower to follow. Manufacturing on the scale to which we are accustomed only started to take off towards the end of the eighteenth century with the dawn of industrial capitalism. This transformed the physical and demographic landscape of the Western world. Factories and widespread industrialisation came to be seen to represent a modern economy. In a relatively short period of time, millions of people moved from the agricultural areas in which their ancestors had lived for centuries to cities to work in these newly constructed edifices, with tools and equipment that their forebears would have found incomprehensible.

Technological innovation was central to these developments. The production of cars on a mass scale, for instance, was greatly enhanced by the use of new machines and production methods in the early 1900s. Only 50 years ago, to walk into a factory in Detroit, Glasgow, Lille, Milan or Cologne was to see many people (mostly blue-collar men) working with machines to mass-produce products ranging from cars to boats, planes and dishwashers, at prices that even most people at the lower end of the income spectrum in Western nations could afford.

If, however, we walk into a manufacturing plant in advanced economies today, a rather different sight confronts us. Overwhelmingly, we see machines doing most of the repetitive work that humans were still doing as late as the 1970s. And the people that we do see walking around the factory floor tend to be highly educated technicians, computer specialists and scientists. Many of them are women with advanced degrees in fields such as engineering.

At the same time, these changes have enabled other developments, most notably in the number of people employed in manufacturing in developed economies. America exemplifies these trends. Between 1979 and 2016, manufacturing jobs in America declined from 19 million in 1979 to about 12 million in 2016. That trend, as well as manufacturing's declining share of overall US GDP, mirrors long term trends in developed nations. Yet that same fall in jobs has gone together with rising manufacturing sector output throughout developed countries, including the United States. Real manufacturing production in America grew by 180% between 1972 and 2007. By 2019, it was back to pre-Great Recession levels. Today America continues to be a major global manufacturer and a priority destination for manufacturing investment.

It is also worth noting that total employment in America grew from 99 million to 151 million throughout the same period, especially in the services sector. Not only did this dwarf the loss of manufacturing jobs, it also meant that millions of individuals who might otherwise have been employed in manufacturing a few decades previously were employed elsewhere.

The reasons for this net manufacturing job decline owes much to America embracing the shift in its comparative advantage towards high-skilled, high-end manufacturing – that is, in imagining, designing, logistics and engineering – while developing countries now have a comparative advantage in unskilled manufacturing tasks, such as assembling the various components. That comparative advantage for America and other developed countries owes much to their edge in technology. Many manufacturing jobs that existed from the 1950s to the 1980s have been replaced by machines, rather than shipped abroad, as advocates of protectionism regularly claim.

But the transition of the working population occasioned by the deployment of ever more sophisticated technology in the manufacturing sector has not been seamless. Not everyone who saw their job in the local factory disappear as a result of technological changes found new employment. Others had to settle for lower wages.

Dissatisfaction with these circumstances has contributed to the upsurge of populist movements in America and Europe. Large segments of blue-collar America and working-class Western Europe have turned to unconventional political figures and movements who have made the reversal of these employment trends in manufacturing a prominent part of their political platform. The changes in the economy's sectoral composition, and associated changes in labour markets, are usually blamed on the lowering of trade barriers and the offshoring of jobs. The solutions proposed invariably involve some form of state intervention. The fact that technological change is estimated to be responsible for anywhere between 80 to 90% of the decline in, for example, American manufacturing jobs is rarely mentioned.

The good news is that, over time, most communities in what is called the Rust Belt have adapted. Of the 185 US counties identified as having a disproportionate share of manufacturing jobs in 1970, approximately 115 had managed to switch successfully away from manufacturing by 2016. Of the other 70, some 40 had exhibited 'strong' or 'emerging' economic performance between 2000 and 2016. Places such as Pittsburgh, for example, can no longer be dismissed as Rust Belt cities.

That said, manufacturing remains a prominent example of how the knock-on effects of technologically driven changes in the economy go beyond economics. In his famous debate with the Marxist historian Eric Hobsbawm, the Oxford economic historian Max Hartwell demonstrated that, thanks to nineteenth-century industrialisation, there were remarkable improvements in overall living standards, lifespans and general health levels throughout the Western world. Yet it is also true that the same transitions, occasioned in part by technology, also helped usher in Marxist and socialist movements determined to undermine the very economic system that was largely responsible for such progress. A similar dynamic is at work today. The transformative effects of technology on manufacturing have generated great wealth and resulted in many people working in far less physically strenuous jobs than their grandparents. But it has also left significant groups feeling abandoned, disenfranchised and wanting to change, through politics, some of the economic dynamics associated with technological change.

A different set of challenges is associated with another sector of the economy that has been transformed by technology. Like contemporary capitalism, the roots of modern banking lie in the medieval period. The financial revolution that occurred during this period produced new legal arrangements such as partnership contracts, accounting tools such as double-entry bookkeeping, and banking devices such as the cheque, the drawing account and the bill of exchange. Above all, it was during the early Middle Ages that Western Europeans came to recognise that money was not simply a means of exchange. Under certain conditions (most notably, those of economic growth), they saw that money could acquire the character of liquid fungible capital. That, in turn, encouraged the advent of new ways of estimating the different risks associated with different uses of capital.

In their own way, these were technological changes. After all, technology goes beyond machines and embraces other tools and instruments by which humans transform the world around them. In the late medieval and early modern worlds of finance, these included economic and legal tools such as life annuities, mutual funds and share ownership in what we would call limited liability corporations. These devices allowed people to mobilise monetary capital in ways that provided the fuel needed by entrepreneurs to transform their ideas into reality. They also allowed those with capital to shift resources quickly to bolster successful initiatives, minimise the losses associated with failed enterprises, and invest in businesses and enterprises whose owners they would never meet in person and whose activities were often carried out thousands of miles away from where most investors lived.

Today the financial sector continues to spur forward economic development in much the same way: by managing risk, investing with an eye to the time-horizon preferred by their clients, and moving capital quickly to those parts of the economy that need it. A world without monetary capital and managed risk would be a very poor world indeed. That said, it is precisely because of the financial sector's pivotal role in modern economies that instability in banking and finance can lead to broader and more systematic economic volatility and therefore political instability. The causes of financial meltdowns and runs on banks can range from bad decisions on the part of its practitioners to a fundamental lack of confidence on the part of large segments of the population in the overall economic lookout. But whatever the causes, problems in the financial sector cannot help but spill over into every other economic sector.

Contemporary technological developments have exacerbated these strengths and potential weaknesses in the financial sector. Technology has, for instance, resulted in ever greater automation of financial activities, ranging from everyday banking services to investments, trading, risk management and insurance. Whether it is banking a cheque on your phone or the application of computer-generated mathematical algorithms by major investment firms engaged in risk assessment, technology has accelerated the speed at which the financial sector performs its vital functions.

New technologies such as the use of smart analytics have, for instance, permitted financial businesses to explore the consumer data at their disposal in ways that enhance the predictive power of their modelling. Other technologies allow real-time financial transactions to occur in ways that once took weeks, thereby diminishing the degree of risk and uncertainty. The ability of banks and financial houses to monitor the performance of their investments has also been dramatically enhanced. Even insurance services are being transformed. Car insurance once focused on indirect indicators – the age of drivers, for instance – to determine insurance premiums. That, however, is being replaced by closer computer analysis of data concerning how, say, certain types of vehicles are used or the impact of weather on patterns of driver behaviour.

Yet for all these improvements, banks continue to fail, hedge funds go bust, mortgage markets collapse, stock markets occasionally behave with bewildering unpredictability, and fraud and financial crimes have not been eliminated. In short, while technology has helped diminish uncertainty and risk in some areas, it has proved incapable of eliminating human fallibility, weakness or our inability to know everything that would allow us to determine far in advance that a particular investment is guaranteed to produce a certain level of return.

There have also been occasions when excessive reliance on new technologies has contributed to spectacular failings in financial markets. Many of the financial instruments developed in the late 1990s and early 2000s were based on quantitative risk modelling for setting capital levels and assessing risk. Much of this modelling was reliant on highly sophisticated risk assessment technology. In many cases, banks and financial enterprises were encouraged to embrace this technology by regulators who believed that it would reduce the potential for extreme upheavals in markets. Use of the same models and technology also meant that many of these banks and financial houses also reacted in the same (mistaken) way when things did not go as predicted. To that extent, excessive reliance on computer-generated models and algorithms meant that prudence and common sense often failed to prevail.

Likewise, technology's contribution to the tremendous speed of contemporary financial transactions and investments can be a double-edged sword. When so much is automated, the potential for the effects of major errors in capital investment or lending to magnify quickly throughout economies and across borders is raised. What took weeks and months during the Great Depression can now take place in hours and days thanks to the speed at which financial information is transmitted. One of the first and most vivid manifestations of this occurred during the 1997 Asian financial crisis as the fallout of a financial meltdown in one country – Thailand – was rapidly transmitted to other Asian nations such as Indonesia, South Korea and Malaysia, because of the increased integration of these financial markets that had been enhanced by technology. Financial contagion, as it came to be called, had a significant technological face.

As in manufacturing, technology has greatly enhanced humanity's capacity to shape the world through banking and finance. Few of us, I suspect, would want to go back to an economic world in which the technologies deployed in the manufacturing and financial sectors remained relatively primitive by our standards. In both instances, though, we also see that new technologies generate as many challenges as opportunities for human betterment.

As Jean Daniélou noted, 'Technology awakens in man a sense of his power.' We cannot, however, know all the effects of the power associated with new technologies. This is all the more reason why the hubris that technology can generate in its human creators needs to be disciplined by such decidedly un-technological virtues of humility, temperance and prudence.

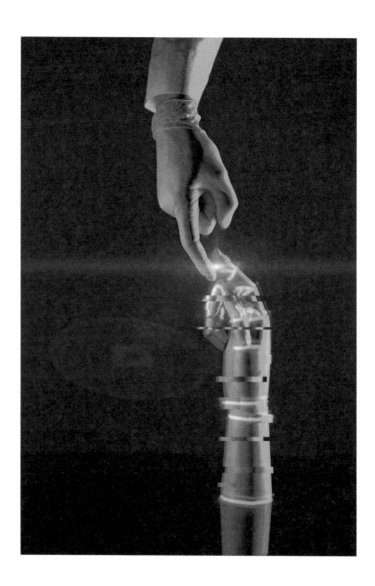

AI can only do what it is told by its author.

ALGORITHMS VS HUMANITY

Andrew Keen

Much thought has been given to the threat of artificial intelligence (AI) to humanity. So, what exactly should 'humanity' mean, and what sort of 'humanism' should we be developing in the age of smart machines? Are there historical precedents for this kind of philosophical humanism, or do we need new kinds of discourses to educate artificially intelligent things?

Artificial intelligence, a term describing computer algorithms that programme smart machines, has become so ubiquitous out here in Silicon Valley that the phrase is used rarely. Just as the word 'water' would be gratuitous to fish if they could speak, so technologists no longer need to talk about 'artificial intelligence' when describing their digital products. AI, you see, is everything and everywhere in Silicon Valley. Digital technology without AI is like an engine without a motor or a human being without a heart. It's a contradiction in terms.

Given that Big Tech *is* smart algorithmic tech, every Silicon Valley company is now an AI company. Google, a networked algorithm that mimics our brain, is perfecting AI-powered search. Apple is the smartphone company now working on an AI car designed to be even smarter than Tesla vehicles. Amazon is automating its warehouses with AI robots that effortlessly do all the heavy lifting. Meta, once a social media company known as Facebook, is pioneering AI-powered smart worlds in the virtual reality of the 'metaverse'. And alongside these multi-trillion-dollar AI multinationals, the office parks of Silicon Valley are teeming with start-ups developing disruptive AI software in everything from law, medicine and engineering to agriculture, finance, human resources and entertainment.

The holy grail for all these tech companies, big and small alike, is to create AI that replaces our physical human labour with the 'work' of the algorithm. That is what tech visionaries eulogise as the disruption of the digital age. Just as Google is replacing the librarian and Apple will replace the driver with their self-driving car, so these tech start-ups – the Apples, Googles and Amazons of our collective AI future – will eventually replace the professional lawyer, the doctor, the accountant, the office worker, the farmer, the engineer, the banker, the politician and, yes, even the essayist.

On second thoughts, maybe there is another reason the term 'artificial intelligence' is not uttered too often in polite company out here in Silicon Valley. AI is what Nietzsche might have defined as an 'all-too-dangerous' word. It imagines a post-human world in which smart machines, rather than you or I, do all the heavy intellectual and physical lifting. AI is designed to make us redundant. That's very nice, of course, if you own the algorithm that reaps the economic rewards of this radical disruption. But what about the rest of us – the former lawyers, doctors, engineers, bankers, office workers, farmers and essayists – those so-called inter-mediaries who, historically, did all the intellectual and physical heavy lifting and have now been 'disintermediated' by the algorithm?

We have a word that collectively describes all these folks. It's the H word: humanity. And, unlike AI, this word has become quite fashion-able these days, particularly outside Silicon Valley. The H word is now in vogue because many of us see humanity as not just a rival but also a potential victim of AI. Marc Andreessen, the original boy genius of Silicon Valley as the co-founder of Netscape and now tech's most influen-tial venture capitalist, famously described software as 'eating the world'. But a more awkward, unpalatable truth is that AI – a potentially post-human smart technology that techno-pessimists warn could be our final invention – might actually be devouring humanity by making us and our labour redundant.

Science fiction writers have been warning us about this for generations. Philip K. Dick's 1968 dystopian novel, *Do Androids Dream of Electric Sheep?*, for example, imagined a dark, dispiriting world in which miserable humans and their equally miserable robots were almost indistinguish-able. The book was turned into Ridley Scott's 1982 cult classic movie *Blade Runner*, a defiantly humanist and memorably cyberpunk critique of both Big Tech and of AI.

So, what sort of humanist thinking should we be pursuing in the age of smart machines? Is humanism compatible with AI? Or do humans need to think of smart digital tech as a species threat? Should we humans be devouring AI before it devours us if we are to protect our humanity in the digital twenty-first century?

We humans have been through this before, of course. Two hundred years ago, industrial technology threatened to eat what the techno-optimistic Karl Marx called the 'idiocy' of rural life. In contrast with Marx, romantic poets such as William Wordsworth and William Blake celebrated and mourned what they considered to be the essential humanity of pre-industrial civilisation. Less poetic agricultural labourers, who we now remember as Luddites, even smashed the machines that threatened their rural livelihoods.

But for Marx, whose education was steeped in the liberationist humanism of the Enlightenment, the technology of the Industrial Revolution promised to liberate us from prosaic labour. As he wrote in his 1856 collection of essays, *The German Ideology,* the potentially cornucopian technology of industrialisation promised to free us from the drudgery of specialised mechanical work. We humans are, Marx believed, naturally a combination of hunters, fishermen, herdsmen and cultural critics. He defined this version of humanity as our 'species-being' and suggested that its essence had been 'alienated' from us by the dehumanising nature of the division of labour, which, he believed, had reached its climax in the factory-based capitalism of nineteenth-century industrial society.

A high-tech post-capitalist world, Marx imagined, could make us whole again. Technology, then, was simultaneously the problem and the solution to the existential crisis of humanity in mid-nineteenth-century capitalist society. Industrial technology was alienating us from ourselves by turning us all into narrow specialists, thereby locking into what the German sociologist, Max Weber, in his 1905 work *The Protestant Ethic and the Spirit of Capitalism*, called 'the iron cage'.

But Marx believed we could break out of this cage by overthrowing the owners of what he called the means of production – which meant the then high-tech industrial factories of the mid-nineteenth century. Rather than wanting to liberate humanity from technology, Marx believed that technology could liberate humanity from the oppressive fate of the working class. Industrial technology, if commonly owned, he believed, could allow us to be fishermen and herdsmen and cultural critics. He described such a state of affairs as a communist society.

'In communist society, where nobody has one exclusive sphere of activity but each can become accomplished in any branch he wishes, society regulates the general production and thus makes it possible for me to do one thing today and another tomorrow,' Marx wrote in *The German Ideology*. 'To hunt in the morning, fish in the afternoon, rear cattle in the evening, criticise after dinner, just as I have a mind, without ever becoming hunter, fisherman, herdsman or critic.'

Marx's vision was to overthrow capitalism and capture the disruptive technology of industrialisation by doing away with private property. In a communist society, technology would be publicly owned and distributed, creating – in his mid-nineteenth-century enlightened mind, at least – the conditions for both material and creative abundancy. Rather than a source of unhappiness and exploitation, work in Marx's revolutionary society would become what he might have described as the 'thing-in-itself' that defined our humanity. By being free to hunt and fish and write whenever we wanted, we would, Marx optimistically predicted, finally realise our humanity.

Now, of course, we know that communist society didn't quite work out as Marx hoped. Technology in Soviet Russia and Maoist China was, indeed, publicly distributed and, in theory at least, collectively owned. But rather than becoming a liberating source that would enrich our meaning as human beings, it actually produced an existential crisis for humanity that rivalled the worst spiritual misery of nineteenth-century industrial society.

The depressing truth about twentieth-century communist society was most memorably captured by George Orwell in his 1949 dystopian novel *Nineteen Eighty-Four*. Orwell's polemic describes the spiritual impoverishment of the human condition in a supposedly revolutionary state, where all technology was monopolised by a repressive dictatorship. Rather than enabling hunting, fishing and the writing of cultural criticism, the cutting-edge technology in *Nineteen Eighty-Four* was deployed by Big Brother to punish any kind of physical or intellectual creativity.

But Orwell's novel didn't represent the end of humanity's doomed love affair with the liberating quality of technology. In 1984, to celebrate the introduction of the Apple Macintosh, their first personal desktop computer, Apple made an infamous television advertisement titled '1984'. Produced by *Blade Runner* director Ridley Scott, the 60-second commercial featured a dismal group of identical male clones, all filmed in black and white, who are liberated by a kaleidoscopic blonde female athlete hurling a sledgehammer.

'On January 24, Apple Computer will introduce Macintosh,' the advertisement, masterminded by Apple CEO Steve Jobs, concluded. 'And you'll see why 1984 won't be like *1984*.'

Think of this advertisement as Jobs' 60-second, Silicon Valley version of Marx's *German Ideology*. Humanity, the commercial suggested, would be radically empowered by the new personal Apple Macintosh computer. The power of personal technology, the commercial promised, would liberate us from mundane tasks and empower all of us to become glamorous authors, musicians and filmmakers.

Some of this was true, of course. The personal computer revolution, begun in 1984 with the Apple Macintosh, has indeed liberated us from many of our most annoying tasks. But the idea that we can now all become authors, musicians and filmmakers through personal technology is as illusionary now as it was then. In fact, the digital revolution has been a catastrophe for the creative industries. There are 50% fewer newspapers and professional journalists in 2022 than there were in 1984, for example. And other twentieth-century creative professions, such as photography or songwriting, have been even worse affected than journalism.

The internet, particularly the Web 2.0 revolution triggered at the turn of the twenty-first century, has only really empowered multi-trillion-dollar multi-nationals such as Google and Facebook. These internet companies have appropriated our private data in exchange for 'free' online products, creating what Shoshana Zuboff has dubbed the age of surveillance capitalism. These Big Tech behemoths have slickly marketed their search engines and social media platforms as public services, and yet they behave with the commercial rapacity that would have shocked capitalism's greatest critic, Karl Marx, himself.

That's the great fear as we teeter on the brink of an AI revolution that is about to revolutionise twenty-first-century life even more radically than the nineteenth-century Industrial Revolution. For all the seductive happy talk by Big Tech marketing departments about the value to humanity of smartphones, smart cars and smart homes, the truth is that the AI revolution will only compound the current winner-take-all architecture of today's digital economy. Fewer and fewer private AI companies will control larger and larger segments of the economy. And the smart technology of these AI oligarchies will destroy more and more conventional twentieth-century jobs in law, medicine, engineering, finance and retail.

So, to borrow some words from one of Marx's most controversial students, V I Lenin: what is to be done? How can we genuinely protect humanity from a rapacious AI revolution that will replace many traditional jobs and labour with smart machines?

Back in 2017, I wrote a book titled *How to Fix the Future*, which laid out a manifesto about reining in Big Tech. Five years later, this manifesto, if anything, is even more relevant. We need much more aggressive governmental regulation to ensure that there is public scrutiny of unaccountable Big Tech companies, especially chilling start-ups like OpenAI. Government needs to take much more responsibility also for instituting radical economic reforms – such as guaranteed basic income – to ensure that history doesn't repeat itself and we return to the Luddite violence of the early nineteenth century.

But we can't rely exclusively on government to protect humanity in the face of today's AI revolution. The problem is that Orwell's *Nineteen Eighty-Four* is very much alive in contemporary China, where the state is leveraging AI to create a digital version of Big Brother. Known as the 'social credit' system, this involves building a giant algorithm for rewarding political loyalty and punishing heresy. Ironically, the Chinese model even disintermediates secret policemen, who will be made mostly redundant by the chilling efficiencies of the system.

An equally important change is rethinking technology's relationship with humanity. The old Enlightenment fallacy, that new technology can liberate humanity, has proven to be profoundly corrosive. Marx was wrong to argue in the *German Ideology* that we, as humans, want to be simultaneously fishermen, herdsmen and cultural critics. One healthy antidote to Marx's romanticised cult of labour is the work of the German twentieth-century political philosopher Hannah Arendt. Her 1958 classic, *The Human Condition*, lays out three kinds of human activities: labour, work and action.

We need to use these three Arendtian categories to prioritise how humans should invest their time in our algorithmic age. An increasingly ubiquitous AI might indeed make both labour and work ultimately redundant for most of humanity. But what about 'action', the most ancient and storied of Arendt's trinity of human activities?

The idea of the computer algorithm was invented by Augusta Ada King, the Countess of Lovelace, an astonishingly brilliant nineteenth-century mathematician who also happened to be Lord Byron's daughter.

Lovelace not only founded the very idea of AI, which she christened 'the analytical engine', but also recognised its fundamental limitation when it came to replicating the human being.

'The Analytical Engine has no pretensions to originate anything,' Lovelace somehow grasped. 'It can do whatever we know how to order it to perform.'

The idea of the algorithm not having the 'pretensions to originate anything' might be the most critical concept uttered in the entire nineteenth century (certainly a million times more valuable than anything Marx wrote). What Lovelace understood is that software can never learn to think for itself. It can only do what it is told by its author. While AI can replicate human activity in two of Arendt's three activities (labour and work), it can never learn 'action'. Human action or agency, then, is a uniquely human quality which will always exist outside the AI realm.

In contrast to many contemporary techno-pessimists who fear we are on the brink of a *Blade Runner* set, in which humans and robots will be indistinguishable, the English writer Jeanette Winterson believes that AI might spark a humanist renaissance in the twenty-first century. Winterson's sparkling 2021 polemic, *12 Bytes*, borrows heavily from Ada Lovelace in arguing that technology can never originate anything. AI, for example, can never come up with an original definition of what it means to be human. Only we human beings can do that. And that is why I'm cautiously optimistic that Winterson's all too human hope about our AI century might not be entirely misplaced.

Still Life with a Salt, Pieter Claesz,
ca. 1640–45.

FOR THE LOVE OF WINE

Bruce Anderson

'Freedom and whisky gang thegither' proclaimed Robbie Burns. The same could surely be said for freedom and wine – indeed, for civilisation and wine. There are, however, ambivalences. At its best, as Robert Louis Stevenson said, 'wine is bottled poetry. But it is not always at its best – or rather, its drinkers are not; Jekyll can turn into Hyde. Wine mirrors the ambivalences of the human condition. All good drink is moreish, but 'more' is not always a good idea. Any oenophile should aspire to claim, with Winston Churchill, that they had taken more out of wine that it had out of them. To express it in even grander terms, those who love wine should hope to anticipate the pleasures of the celestial regions while keeping original sin at bay.

That might seem a miraculous harmony, but miracles and wine can also go together, as in Christ's first miracle, during the marriage at Cana. That had two notable aspects. First, it concerned wine. Second, the account in John's Gospel shows the Virgin Mary in a new light. This is not the tremulous girl of the Annunciation, nor is it the Mater Dolorosa of the Crucifixion. This is the Yiddishe Mama of yore, brushing aside her son's disclaimer and generally giving orders all round. A charming scene which led to a jolly wedding feast, a happy and untypical interlude before the journey to Gethsemane, and to Golgotha.

Yet there was an earlier non-divine miracle which also involved wine. Although the miracle workers' names will remain unknown, at least in this world, it was one of the great prehistoric agricultural discoveries. There is a story which is often read to small children, about a farmer whose pigsty caught fire, killing all the animals. The farmer, very upset, touched one of the carcases and then thrust his burned finger into his mouth, to cool it off. There was a delicious taste. As time went on, the farmer and his friends realised that they did not have to burn down the pigsty in order to enjoy roast pork.

There must be a parallel with wine. When the delicious grapes had ripened, it would not have been possible to eat them all at once. Some would have been stored, in hollowed-out tree trunks or even in primitive earthenware vessels. As a result, many of them would have been crushed. When this was discovered a few months later, the negligent fellow who did the storing might have been in big trouble, until someone tasted the resulting fermented juice.

The earliest wine was made from wild vines. But some time between 8000 and 5000 BC (the archaeologists are still arguing about the dates) in modern Turkey, Syria and Georgia, vines were cultivated. This practice spread gradually throughout the Eastern Mediterranean and was associated with the growth of trade. In Thucydides's words: 'The peoples of the Mediterranean began to emerge from barbarism when they learned to cultivate the olive and the vine.'

From early on, the fruits of the vine were associated with religion. The fall of the year, the life-threatening harshness of winter, the rebirth of life-giving fertility in the spring: explanations for these phenomena were at the core of most ancient religions. The death and rebirth of Osiris, the kidnapping of Proserpine followed by her partial release – it seems certain that in the mind of the ancients, this would be connected to the destruction of grapes, followed by their resurrection as wine. Scholars are still arguing about what actually happened during the Eleusinian Mysteries, the annual initiation ceremonies held by the cult of Demeter. That secret cult was good at keeping its secrets. There have even been suggestions that its initiates developed early forms of hallucinogenic drugs. But it seems self-evident that in rituals to glorify Demeter, Proserpine and the fertility of the earth, wine would have been included.

It certainly formed a crucial part of Jewish ceremonies, such as Passover. As well as Jesus, who produced the first great wine, Cana grand cru, Judaism also supplied the first wine-drinking hypocrite. After everything that he had gone through – stuck on a boat with all those beasts – Noah could hardly be blamed for getting sloshed. On one occasion, he ended up in his tent, no doubt snoring his head off, and naked. His son Ham saw him thus unattired. This was hardly a crime on the scale of Susannah and the Elders, but when Noah came to, no doubt in the grip of a stonking hangover, he cursed Ham and his posterity. That was poor behaviour on his part.

We know more about the ceremonies associated with Dionysus and Bacchus – the same Gods in different languages. Dionysiac and Bacchanalian: the words survive to describe events which lead up to drunkenness, licentiousness and general mayhem, concluding in orgies. The end of the evening would have resembled a cross between Oxford's Bullingdon Club and Leicester Square on a Saturday night. Nudity would have spread well beyond Noah. In both Athens and Rome, the authorities made attempts to suppress or at least regulate these outbreaks of misrule. That prig Livy was especially disapproving, but versions of the bacchanals survived until the Christians were able to suppress paganism.

A quarter of a millennium before that, a great emperor, Antoninus Pius, commissioned the finest ever architectural tribute to the glories of the grape. In what is now Lebanon, his magnificent Temple of Bacchus still stands as part of the temple complex at Baalbek, in the Bekaa Valley, which is appropriate for two reasons. First, wine has been cultivated there from earliest times, probably more than 3,000 years before Antoninus Pius's benefaction; indeed, it still is. At least three major chateaux, Ksara, Massaya and Musar, have continued to produce serious wine during the worst of Lebanon's travails. The vignerons must be fed up with jokes about a touch too much cordite in the '09. Second, here again the pleasures of the human condition are juxtaposed with its horrors. One of Massaya's best wines is *Les Terrasses de Baalbeck*. The vineyard overlooks the temples. It also overlooks the Hezbollah encampment across the road. Thus far, there has been peaceful coexistence. But the Hezbollah lot regularly fire off a few rounds, a *feu de joie* as it were, just to remind everyone that we are in Lebanon. The wines of Bekaa travel well: the joie of Hezbollah less so.

Today, officially, Islamic cultures are hostile to alcohol, which is surprising, given the Koran's extensive borrowings from the Talmud. Some experts claim that only two or three verses in the Koran do refer to wine, and that they concentrate on denouncing intoxication. The art of the Islamic world does not always show the same aversion. In some of the Omayyad hunting lodges in Northern Jordan, there are frescoes. After a strenuous day's chase, contented-looking chaps are relaxing while diaphanously clad women bring round trays of goblets. It is unlikely that those goblets contained Diet Coke. But in later centuries, puritanism triumphed, though often mitigated by hypocrisy.

Christianity followed Judaism in its use of wine. It is central to the Eucharist: 'This is my blood of the New Testament, which is shed for many for the remission of sins.' Is there a more dramatic, more moving phrase in any literature or liturgy? Almost thou persuadest me to be a Christian. Yet there is a problem. Tertullian encouraged his fellow Christians to set a good example to their pagan neighbours, who would then marvel at 'how these Christians love one another'. That might have been true in the Gospel of Perfection, but it never existed. For centuries, Christians were ready to slay other Christians for taking a different view of the Gospel of Love. Christ allowed his blood to be shed, as he proclaimed during the first Eucharist, but soon his followers were spilling each other's. Around the time of the Reformation, there were fierce arguments over the nature of the Eucharist. Was it Transubstantiation, Consubstantiation or merely symbolic? In those conflicts, Christian blood was shed and Christian flesh was tortured and burned. Christians are heirs to a great spiritual, intellectual and aesthetic heritage. Music, art, architecture, glorious language, profound theology and, above all, redemption; Christ's Cross is their salvation. Yet still, 'The troubles of our proud and angry dust/Are from eternity, and shall not fail,' as A. E. Housman put it. The wine of the Eucharist inspired sin, as well as forgiveness.

Wine is also the handmaiden of talk. As the evening unfolds, that can range across a wide horizon, from profundity to nonsense. In my experience, it is helpful if everyone imbibes at roughly the same rate. Then all jokes are funny, all banalities are insights.

I developed a lifelong love affair with wine at the University of Cambridge in the late 1960s and early 70s. Although college cellars had been nurtured by pastoral care from generations of dons, undergraduates were sometimes allowed access, at bargain prices. In those days, most colleges had fellows who felt that there was enough scholarship already in their chosen discipline so that any contribution from them would be otiose and they could concentrate on being good college men. That role included teaching undergraduates, usually very well, and often entertaining them, often generously. Any Platonism almost always remained Platonic.

These men's tastes had been formed when good wine was cheap. As prices began to rise, there were complaints. I remember one elderly don almost calling for sackcloth and ashes. 'If you ever want to drink anything decent, you young men will simply have to become – there was a pause before his whole frame shuddered and he emitted a howl of lamentation

– 'bankers'. His wine merchant had just told him that the latest vintage of Latour would cost £60 a case.

There were also bargains elsewhere. In those days, the University Arms hotel was a hideous modern excrescence: a disgrace to its name. (It has since been replaced by something a bit better.) Once, I was walking back to college when the heavens opened. To avoid inundation, I darted into the hotel, the nearest thing to an Ark, looked with disfavour on a pint of gaseous beer and picked up the wine list with no expectation of pleasure, just for something to read. Blow me: 1945 Latour and the same vintage of Lafite, seven pounds ten shillings each. I phoned an oenophile chum and discarded the beer. We ate the simplest food, something like cold roast beef, that the kitchen could not ruin. The wines were *sans pareil*. A few days later, we thought that we would repeat the experience. I called the hotel to book a table and ask the sommelier to open the wines when he thought it appropriate. 'Sorry, Sir, those bottles are no longer available.' Looking back, our enthusiasm during the first innings probably set off alarm bells and led someone to do some checking. How maddening. Talk about sackcloth and ashes.

A couple of years ago, I had the pleasure of tasting the '45 Latour once again, courtesy of Simon Berry at Berry Bros. It was majestic. I would be tempted to compare it to the highest peak in a massive mountain range or to Durham Cathedral seen from below. But attempts to describe great wine in words almost always fail and often read like parodies. Perhaps one should restrict description to a single phrase: the finest wine that I have ever tasted.

In the 1980s, I was lucky enough to spend a lot of time in the US. The Americans were still discovering wine and, as a result, residual naivety created bargains. In the great year of 1980 – I was on current affairs TV business – I had been using the 1976 Pontet-Canet as a table wine in one hotel. P-C had not yet acquired its super-Fifth Growth status, and that was a light vintage. But it was ready to drink, pleasant, and cheap. The inevitable moment came. A waiter announced: 'Sorry, Sir, we've run out of that.' As I reached for the wine list to find a substitute, he continued: 'We do have an earlier year left. Don't suppose you'd be interested.' 'What year?' '1966.' That was a much better vintage. I tried not to look eager while saying casually: 'Knock a couple of bucks off the price and I'll give it a go.' Great fun which also applied to homegrown American bottles.

In 1980, high UK interest rates had sent the pound to around $2.40 and a lot of Washington restaurants had not yet learned to prize Californian wines. It was a good time to discover them. Alas, after Ronald Reagan's apotheosis, the Californians hit town. Their wines became deservedly fashionable and inevitably dearer. Although many of them would still have been too young, the older vintages were quickly consumed, and their replacements were as ready as green strawberries. Meanwhile, the British government had understood the need to relax monetary policy. By early 1982, the pound was virtually at parity with the dollar. In Washington, there was still plenty of good wine, but the bargains had gone.

In South Africa, one could also benefit from a weak currency while observing a fascinating and wonderful country beset by anfractuosity, oscillating between hope and tragedy. In the Cape, abetted by Huguenot immigrants, they had been making wine for 300 years. Around Stellenbosch and Franschhoek, with vineyards surrounded by mountains, the scenery is achingly beautiful.

I spent many evenings in gardens near Stellenbosch, praising the excellent bottles as we tried to work out how South Africa could move to majority rule without sliding into chaos. That quest continues. Some would argue that even thinking about South African wine was escapism and that all energies ought to have been devoted to politics. But as a Russian Grand Duke is reported to have said, between the revolution and the firing squad, there is always time for a bottle of champagne – or, in this case, Cabernet Sauvignon. Housman wrote a light but also serious poem, in which the first line reads: 'Could man be drunk for ever.' In that case, we gather, all would be well:

But men at whiles are sober
And think by fits and starts,
And when they think they fasten
Their hands upon their hearts.
There was, and is, plenty of that in South Africa.

But there are more relaxed regions. Five years ago, I visited Gagnard-Delagrange, an excellent Burgundian wine grower where we were enticed with a 1980 Chassagne-Montrachet premier cru. It had been made by the great Jacques Gagnard, now dead. His daughter,

Marie-Josephine, approaching 80, presided with an authoritative twinkle. She sent her grandson to the cellar to fetch the wine, bottled before he was born.

We were worried; 1980 was not an outstanding year. Would the wine have survived? The colour was yellower than seemed healthy. What would one say if it had died in the bottle? The atmosphere was more tense than the matriarch realised. But our anxieties were wholly unjustified. The wine was delicious. Oh, we of little faith. In the most civilised region on earth, the tasting had turned into an epiphany: another tribute to the glory of Burgundy, and to the good sense of the Psalmist:

And wine that maketh glad the heart of man.
May that continue, world without end, Amen.

A GDR border soldier looking through a camera
towards the Western side of the Berlin Wall, 1988.

WHO'S WATCHING YOU AND WHY?

Elisabeth Braw

Four years ago, a nifty Chinese video-sharing app named TikTok had 55 million monthly users. By January 2022, it had more than one billion. Few people can resist TikTok's viral fun; indeed, people don't even seem to care that recording videos can be incredibly time-consuming and brings little reward except attention. They're hooked. Almost everyone, in fact, gets dopamine highs when using social media and other apps. That addiction makes many disregard the fact that by using apps they are giving away personal data, and that data is extraordinarily useful to others. A culture of consumerism is clashing with a trend towards more government surveillance, especially by regimes that are up to no good.

One of the subjects I focus on is East Germany. People often wonder why I would devote so much time to a country that no longer exists and that was despised even during its brief life. But it is only 32 years since East Germany's demise. Many of today's Germans grew up there, spent their formative years there, and had short or long careers there before their country was inserted into the West German system and they had to begin anew. Like many other citizens of countries behind the Iron Curtain, they had experiences the rest of us will never have.

My focus on East Germany has, however, turned out to be surprisingly relevant in other ways too. In my book *God's Spies*, I chronicle the Stasi's phenomenally successful recruitment of pastors as spies – spies with a mission to keep a constant eye on their friends, acquaintances, parishioners and fellow clergy. Like many other unofficial Stasi collaborators, pastors delivered huge amounts of information and thus helped the Stasi establish an all-encompassing picture of their countrymen. East Germans, unsurprisingly, hated this constant snooping, just like Soviet citizens hated the KGB's snooping and Poles hated that of the SB Ministry of Public Security. Around the world, the Stasi has come to symbolise surveillance. And around the world, people are relieved that this infamous secret police force is safely confined to the dustbin of history.

But surveillance is returning. It has sneaked up on modern society not through a sinister plan, but because modern society is so digitised. Facebook (now known as Meta) makes its fortune by monitoring its users' every post, like, comment and movement, and selling ads based on this information. Facebook Messenger and Instagram, which Facebook also owns, join Facebook as the world's top three data-collecting apps. Thanks to this data collection, users get adverts miraculously targeted to their interests and their location. Because this information is valuable to advertisers, Facebook makes staggering amounts of money: last year, $118 billion, up from $86 billion in 2020.

I boycott Facebook because I believe its algorithms promote division within our societies. But I do use WhatsApp, which is owned by Facebook (now known as Meta), and I use other apps. All of them collect data about me. WhatsApp, for example, collects information about my purchases, my finances, my location, my contacts, and much else. In fact, almost every app collects troves of information about its users. (Signal Messenger, which collects no personal data, is a rare exception.) These days, any user can find out which information each app collects about them by checking the app's details on Apple's App Store; and yet internet use keeps growing.

Already in 2018, researchers at the University of Oxford's Reuters Institute for the Study of Journalism found that apps sold users' details to an average of ten other companies. Users, though, seem fine with this arrangement, because the resulting ads don't bother them and because they like their apps' convenience (and the mostly non-existing fee). Besides, they may say, what's the harm in a company knowing every detail about their lives? At a recent conference, I raised the issue of companies' collection of consumer data in a discussion with a senior politician from a digitally sophisticated European country. He had no concerns about being a *gläserner Mensch* (transparent individual). 'I don't care if the *Financial Times* can find out, based on my data, where I am and reports on its front page tomorrow that I'm at this conference,' he said. He would not be important enough to merit a scoop on the FT's front page, but you get the idea. People aren't too bothered about companies knowing everything about them because, unlike the Stasi, companies are seen as having benign motives. And even though they know that the companies they use share their data with other companies, they're still fine with it, because companies simply want to make money.

Sometimes, users' constant connectedness becomes a national security risk. 'Our phones know basically everything about us,' Staffan Truvé, CTO and co-founder of the cyber threat intelligence firm Recorded Future, told me. 'When Russia was getting ready to invade Ukraine, observers in the rest of the world could figure it out because the soldiers had their phones with them and all of a sudden there was immense phone activity in the areas where they were being posted.' Russian law forbids soldiers from uploading sensitive information on social media, but the troops could still be spotted thanks to their phones. But even when internet users aren't part of a massive troop movement to encircle a smaller neighbour, their connectedness and digital trail raise red flags.

Why are we comfortable with Facebook and sundry other companies knowing every detail about our lives when the Stasi's less extensive knowledge still fills the world with dread and outrage? Primarily because it's a convenience. What's more, most companies promise users a better experience if they leave their cookies on; users get ads targeted to their interests rather than generic ones. If having to view ads is part of the deal, why not view ones that are at least relevant to one's interests? They are, of course, relevant because they are based on the user's data. Apps, in turn, are said to need to capture a certain amount of personal information in order to function.

The internet-fuelled convenience of daily life has already made most of us less sensitive to surveillance. Oddly, even Western politicians who are passionately opposed to anything resembling 'Big Brother government' are happy to allow companies to know about their lives in detail. I know this because said politicians use social media.

But what happens if that data lake – or, more accurately, data ocean – doesn't stay with the companies to which consumers give their data, or even with their commercial partners? What if, say, government decided to get access to it? The Stasi's enormous files and wall charts mapping people's connections would look like child's play.

That's already happening. For years now, law enforcement agencies have trawled through suspects' internet activity as part of investigations into crimes ranging from murders to terrorist atrocities. In 2012, two thirds of law enforcement officers believed that social media helped solve crimes more quickly, and 80% accessed social media as part of their investigations. The police can, for example, ask Facebook for access to a specific user's activity. Between January and June of 2021, UK law enforcement agencies made 10,678 such requests to Facebook, 88% of which the company complied with. Indeed, companies are obliged to comply with most information requests made by Western governments, as the requests can only be made with the aid of a subpoena or another court authorisation. It's the rule of law in action.

But other governments are keen on internet users' data too, and not just for criminal investigations. One such government is already delivering a masterclass in how the state can tap into its country's tech sector – and thus into the personal data of any internet user. In November 2021, China enacted legislation called the Personal Identification Protection Law (PIPL), a Chinese version of the EU's GDPR. Like GDPR, PIPL has extraterritorial reach; that is, it applies around the world. As PWC notes in a November 2021 advisory, 'If your company processes any personal data from China to provide a product or service to Chinese residents or to analyse their behaviour, you will likely have to comply with PIPL's rules – even if you have no business presence in China.' Also, like GDPR, PIPL obliges companies to keep a safe inventory of consumer data to make sure it's not accessed by people and groups who have no business viewing it; say, hackers. But unlike the EU's institutions, the Chinese government can also demand access to consumer data. In 2017, China implemented its National Intelligence Law, which obliges citizens, organisations and companies to support the government's intelligence-gathering.

The significance of these two laws for the internet age is obvious: companies have an obligation to provide Chinese authorities with the massive amounts of user data they collect. Chinese companies are under particular pressure. In countries including the United States, legislators have woken up to the fact that companies that were until recently considered simply another part of the commercial sector – social media platforms focused on teenagers, say – may now pose national security challenges. In late 2021, the US Senate Commerce Committee questioned executives at popular app companies including TikTok, which is owned by Beijing-based ByteDance. The TikTok executive, head of public policy Michael Beckerman, chose his words carefully. 'We do not share information with the Chinese government,' he said. He didn't promise, though, that the company would never share such information, and indeed he could make no such promise. A recent study found that TikTok, Facebook's successor as the world's social media darling, is extraordinarily active in sharing user data with third parties, and that there is no way for the user to know where their data ends up. Should Chinese authorities request the data, TikTok would not be in a position to refuse.

For Chinese authorities, the trail left by users young and old, famous and non-famous, from all walks of life, would be a treasure trove in its surveillance of people, including exiled Chinese citizens and foreigners. What Beijing is willing and able to do when it comes to surveillance of individuals and entire population groups is already on display in Xinjiang province, where Uighurs are constantly watched by tools including government cameras and a commonly used Koran prayer app.

Even if TikTok executives are personally eager to safeguard users' data, they need only look at what has happened in recent months to Chinese tech executives who have demonstrated independence from Beijing. In November, the Chinese government imposed massive fines on tech giants Alibaba and Tencent for alleged monopoly practices. Last autumn, it also emerged that Beijing plans to break up Alibaba's payment system, Alipay, a low-cost alternative to credit cards that can now be used in shops around the world, including the US nationwide chain CVS.

Indeed, Alibaba and Tencent are unlikely to now refuse Chinese government requests for user data. The same goes for DiDi, a Beijing-based ride-share company that has been expanding internationally at a rapid pace and narrowing the gap with industry leader Uber. By 2016 DiDi had become so successful that Uber withdrew from China and sold its operations to DiDi in exchange for a stake in the firm. But as was the case with Alibaba and Tencent, DiDi's success made Beijing think the company was becoming too powerful – and therefore too independent. In December 2021, less than half a year after its triumphant entry on the New York Stock Exchange, DiDi withdrew following a Chinese government announcement that the firm would be banned from app stores in China for 'privacy violations'. It is undoubtedly clear to DiDi, too, that it would be unadvisable to defy the Chinese government. And now that Beijing has set the tone, sundry authoritarian governments of smaller countries are likely to follow its example.

This should concern every internet user. You might say, I'm not an important person, so it doesn't matter if the Chinese government or any other government gets my user data. True. But many so-called unimportant people work for companies or government agencies that a foreign government might be interested in. A junior intelligence analyst or nuclear engineer, for example, might take DiDi for various errands, perhaps including visits to gambling shops or red light districts. A government official's daily life can be tracked using his or her Alipay transactions. And TikTok, of course, knows virtually every detail of more than one billion people's lives. Such information is a gold mine for intelligence agencies, which in past years deployed intelligence officers to painstakingly map out a potential agent's life before approaching them, as did the Stasi with its informants.

The realisation that Beijing could tap into internet user data for intelligence purposes prompted, in 2019, a rare intervention by CFIUS, the US overseer of investments and acquisitions by foreign companies. The year before, the Chinese firm Kunlun had completed a takeover of Grindr, a dating app popular with gay men. CFIUS, which focuses on foreign takeovers' national security risks, hadn't paid any attention to the acquisition. Soon afterwards, though, CFIUS realised the potential for Chinese government snooping on Grindr users' data – including HIV status and sexual preferences. If Chinese authorities requested access to Grindr data – which the takeover made possible – such users, who might be government officials or hold private-sector posts where they have access to important information, would be vulnerable to blackmail by Beijing. CFIUS forced a reversal of the acquisition. As for those many people who don't work with anything remotely sensitive, it is also useful for a government such as China's to have a complete picture of how individuals, population groups and entire societies lead their lives.

China isn't the only country that has discovered how consumer technology can be used for surveillance. Pegasus powerfully demonstrates another way in which governments can keep track of any person on the planet or, to be precise, anyone with a smartphone. The Israeli company that made and sells Pegasus insists that it's used only for worthy reasons, such as fighting terrorism. But the Pegasus spyware can be remotely installed by any buyer on any smartphone owner's phone, without the targeted person needing to do anything or even noticing that anything is being done. Then the installer – Pegasus's customers are thought to include the governments of Azerbaijan, Bahrain, Hungary, India, Kazakhstan, Mexico, Morocco, Rwanda, Saudi Arabia and the United Arab Emirates – can follow the targeted person's every activity via the smartphone. Journalists, human rights activists and business executives have all unknowingly been kept under surveillance by Pegasus-using governments. Another recent victim was Princess Haya, whose own ex-husband – Dubai's ruler, Sheikh Mohammed bin Rashid Al Maktoum – monitored her using Pegasus.

The future offers plenty of other opportunities for companies and authoritarian governments to keep an all-seeing eye on groups and individuals alike. A taste of that future arrived in 2022 when the upscale supermarket chain Whole Foods (owned by Amazon) premiered a fully digital supermarket. Shoppers simply enter the shop, where overhead computer-vision cameras, weight sensors and deep-learning technology watch their every move and register which items they put in their shopping basket. They can even exit the store without using a payment device, because upon arrival they scan their fingerprints. It's an extremely convenient way of shopping that involves no interaction with another human being but does involve a massive data trail. And the more IoT – the internet of things – expands, the more personal data ends up with a company, possibly other companies, and possibly sundry governments. Consider, for example, the 'smart toys' that parents increasingly like to buy their children in the hope that they will make them smarter. The jury is still out on whether such products aid cognitive development, but what is certain is that they capture massive amounts of data. And so do voice assistants, led by Alexa. Where does the data go? The user has no control.

East Germans developed clever methods to avoid being overheard by the Stasi. If they needed to discuss something sensitive with a friend, they took a walk outside. If the discussion needed to happen indoors, they turned on loud music to make sure any microphones would be unable to pick up the conversation. Indeed, people living under authoritarian regimes have always managed to at least partly outwit the secret police. But how to outwit the internet? The first step is, of course, to want to outwit it. Many twenty-first century citizens of Western countries will continue to tolerate their data being used, because they want to keep enjoying the pleasures of the internet. Others, though, may conclude that giving data away to be used in unknown ways is highly unsettling – and that they should reduce their data donation. In 2020, people spent a daily average of 145 minutes on social media alone, up from 90 minutes ten years earlier. Reducing the time spent interacting with digital devices would improve their mental health and reduce the risk of surveillance by corporates and governments. That's surely a win-win.

Aerial reconnaissance before introduction of
aerial cameras, ca. 1870.

SPIES AS AGENTS OF PEACE

Joshua Rovner

Spies have a terrible reputation. As agents of deception and theft, they arouse suspicion and anger wherever they go. States that employ spies risk a hostile response, suggesting that espionage is a precursor to war. Perhaps this is one reason why they have been held in such disdain for so long. Ancient Greek generals were heroic figures; ancient Greek spies were subject to torture and execution. The Arabic tradition viewed foreign agents as beneath contempt, and the Arabic word for spies, *jasous*, was originally a slur. The French word *espion* was a pejorative in *Ancien Régime* France, associating spies with *agents provocateurs* who destabilised governments and opened the door to foreign aggression. The Catholic and Anglican churches formerly referred to the day before Passover as 'Spy Wednesday', in commemoration of Judas Iscariot's efforts to see how much money he could receive for betraying Jesus. Historians have linked enthusiasm for espionage to rapacious authoritarian regimes such as the Mauryan and Mogul Empires. Their leaders found inspiration in Kautilya's *Arthashastra*, which includes ruthless recommendations on the dark arts.

The presence of spies sparks fear of invasion, and spy scares have a long history. Fear of fifth columnists and saboteurs abounded in France and Britain during the Hundred Years' War. Fears of German espionage roiled Great Britain before the First World War. Fear of British espionage led to a panic in the Soviet Union in the interwar period, culminating in a brief but intense war scare in 1927. Fear of communist infiltration animated McCarthyism in the United States in the early Cold War, causing some to worry that a hot war was coming. In these and other cases, spies were viewed as both sinister and repugnant. No surprise, then, that they rarely received the protections afforded to diplomats or prisoners of war.

For liberal statesmen at the turn of the twentieth century, the antidote to secret intelligence was transparent diplomacy. Transparency alone would not guarantee international stability, but it would make it easier for leaders to work together. Resisting the urge to hoard secrets helps reduce fear that others are cheating on agreements, shirking their obligations or plotting military aggression. International institutions, not secret intelligence agencies, were the safest places to gather information. National security did not flow from espionage and subterfuge but from open diplomacy. It is no accident that Woodrow Wilson's post-war vision rested on 'Open covenants of peace, openly arrived at'. Of his 14 points, this was the first and most vital.

Statesmen, however, proved to be hypocrites. They condemned the practice of espionage while engaging in it with great energy. This was true during Wilson's time, and long before it. Indeed, this hypocrisy preceded the development of modern intelligence agencies by millennia: the ancients spied on each other all the time despite their expressions of moral outrage. Early modern Europeans treated spying as reprehensible, while simultaneously developing the rudiments of intelligence tradecraft. Indeed, some scholars have suggested that the birth of the bureaucratic state in Europe was closely tied to the need for more reliable methods of gathering and organising secret information. In this respect, spying and state-building were linked from the start. Modern liberal democracies have engaged in covert action repeatedly, perhaps believing that it is a necessary stopgap against illiberal regimes. Leaders have also rationalised their activities by distinguishing military scouting from espionage. Only rarely have they acknowledged the nature of their business. Sir James Harris, the eighteenth-century English ambassador to The Hague, was resigned to the necessity of spying though he was clearly not happy about it. 'I abhor this dirty work,' Harris wrote, 'but when one is employed to sweep chimneys one must black one's fingers.'

Statesmen thus have a strange relationship with spies and spying. Many view intelligence agents as little more than glorified thieves, and they have long worried that espionage cuts against earnest efforts to make peace. Yet they find espionage irresistible, and they have built increasingly large and sophisticated intelligence bureaucracies in the name of national security.

Scholars are similarly divided. Whether intelligence is a force for peace and security, or a source of crisis and war, remains an open question. Some warn that intelligence is dangerous because it is difficult to distinguish espionage from war preparations. The targets of intelligence cannot be certain that their rivals simply want to gather information. Very often the tradecraft used to learn more about a foreign state is the same as the tradecraft used to lay the groundwork for military action. The target, then, might fear the worst when it uncovers espionage efforts on its own soil. This is an intelligence twist on the security dilemma, the notion that one state's attempt to improve security makes its rivals feel less secure. Spying might help one state feel better by improving its awareness of rival capabilities and intentions, but the act of spying is unsettling. Observers have recently warned that cyberspace is particularly prone to this problem, because the tools and techniques used to exfiltrate digital information are also prerequisite to cyberspace attack. Attempts to penetrate an adversary's nuclear command, control and communications network are especially risky.

In addition, espionage sometimes reveals opportunities for attack. Such knowledge is tempting, especially if the state believes that its information advantage is a wasting asset. Good intelligence encourages hope of a quick decisive victory over an unsuspecting enemy, and fear of missing out. The goal of intelligence agencies is asymmetric knowledge – one side gains the other's secrets while protecting its own – but this asymmetry encourages opportunistic violence. Israel launched the Six-Day War, for example, in part because it had excellent intelligence on Arab armies.

But in other circumstances, espionage may be a force for peace. Suppose, for instance, that lousy information is a cause of instability. Conflict is costly so states should rationally seek to avoid it, yet they do not know enough about the balance of power to arrive at reasonable compromises. Unequal access to information also makes it difficult for states to commit to peace, because they have a sensible fear of being the sucker. Intelligence agencies could resolve this problem by making critical information available to policy makers and diplomats on all sides. Private information asymmetries that inhibit peaceful bargaining will disappear if peacetime adversaries maintain a competent and productive intelligence bureaucracy. Armed with reasonable knowledge, they will not have to take up arms.

Intelligence might also help resolve the security dilemma, which has more to do with uncertain intentions than with the objective balance of power. States might have good information about adversary forces, but little insight into how adversaries plan to use them. Espionage that reveals this knowledge might help alleviate the problem, reducing the risk of war by misperception or miscalculation. War is more likely when information is hidden and obscure; intelligence agencies are in the business of finding it so that decision makers are not operating in the dark. States are less likely to lash out if they have a reasonable understanding of their rivals.

None of this is to suggest that intelligence collection leads to friendly relations. What it does suggest is that espionage can channel political rivalries away from violence. War is less likely if states are locked in an intelligence contest among dedicated secret services. Spy-versus-spy battles preclude actual battles. States might tolerate foreign espionage because they understand that the alternative is much worse. During the Cold War, the United States and the Soviet Union grudgingly accepted that spying was inevitable, and intelligence professionals on both sides developed 'rules of the game' about acceptable and unacceptable methods. In some cases, they went further, allowing their rivals to act covertly and giving them the benefit of plausible deniability. Allowing the other side to operate in the shadows served as a good way of controlling escalation. Covert action was a useful release valve.

States also advertise their intelligence capabilities to disabuse rivals of the idea that they can remain hidden. This should give would-be aggressors a moment of pause. Sometimes states surveil their rivals – and quietly let them know about it – to reduce their enthusiasm for war and military escalation. In other cases they reveal intelligence in public, as in the ongoing Ukraine crisis, where US leaders have sought to remove Russia's ability to manufacture a phoney pretext for war. Military plans depending on deception and surprise should become less appealing if planners cannot operate in the shadows.

Finally, secret services can serve as conduits for subterranean diplomacy among adversaries who find it difficult to negotiate in public. They can search for signs that long-time rivals are interested in better relations, and set up back channels that might lead to meaningful talks. Domestic hawks usually bash policy makers for reaching out to states they view as implacably hostile. In order to prevent these critics from becoming diplomatic spoilers, secret intelligence services facilitate quiet talks that let the air out of crises. Because they spy on each other, they know each other. The information channels they create to steal information are also useful for sharing it.

Intelligence sometimes lends stability to international relations. Sometimes it makes things worse. How do we know when spying leads to war or peace?

One possible answer has to do with innovation and technology, both of which are topics of enduring interest in the intelligence world. Espionage has always relied on clever technologies for stealing secrets and for avoiding revelation of its activities. Intelligence agencies try to gain access to valuable information without being discovered. But the more valuable the information, the higher the risk of discovery, because states pay closest attention to their dearest secrets. The consequences are especially dire for individuals who spy on behalf of foreign intelligence agencies. Other costs of discovery include the loss of control of sources and methods, which can leave secret services in the dark, or vulnerable to deception. Most relevant here is the danger that revelation of spying activities can lead to unnerving diplomatic crises.

States often turn to technology to reduce these risks. Reliance on technological collection platforms, as opposed to human sources, reduces the physical risk to intelligence personnel. Innovative concealment techniques – from camouflage to codes – protect sources and methods from exposure. And some technologies permit collection from very long distances. Because they are less intrusive, they might be less provocative. Ideally, distant platforms allow intelligence agencies to collect important information about the balance of power without inadvertently causing a crisis. In this way, intelligence technology can ease the problem of misperception and reduce the danger of war.

This argument is appealing. It is logically coherent and consistent with day-to-day international relations. States are hostile to foreign agents trying to recruit human sources, but they usually seem less upset by the notion that foreign satellites are watching them from long distances. Perhaps there is an unspoken acknowledgement that states can keep an eye on one another, as long as they do it from afar. Less intrusive collection methods are less irritating. And sometimes states even welcome this kind of collection, as it gives them an opportunity to show off new capabilities without having to parade them publicly. Doing so bolsters deterrence by quietly revealing their military strength.

Yet there are limits to this logic. One is the historical record. States try very hard to conceal their activities, contriving elaborate camouflage schemes and creative efforts to misdirect foreign observers. These efforts benefit from secrets elicited from foreign spies. In the late 1970s, for example, the Soviet Union deliberately targeted US defence contractors for this purpose. Such activities are inconsistent with the idea that states understand the value of foreign surveillance, much less that they welcome it.

In more extreme cases, there have been attempts to destroy adversaries' distant platforms. This has led to a peculiar sort of arms race, as states invest in new technologies that allow them to collect from ever greater distances, while their targets invest in technologies to stop them. In the late eighteenth century, for example, states started to use hot-air balloons for battlefield observation. Military commanders liked the idea of being able to see behind enemy lines, but there were practical limits to what early balloons could accomplish. Nineteenth-century innovations increased the altitude and manoeuvrability of balloons, yet they were still large and slow and inherently vulnerable. The First World War saw the use of powered flight, which allowed for more aggressive collection, but defenders soon developed tactics that made overhead reconnaissance a very dangerous trade. A similar story played out in the Second World War, when increasingly higher altitude aircraft met increasingly long-range defences.

The technology race continued into the Cold War. Seeking information about Soviet military and economic activities, the United States developed very high-altitude aircraft such as the U-2, an aeroplane that some believed was invulnerable to interception. It was not. In 1960, Soviet forces shot down an American U-2 and captured the pilot, causing a diplomatic crisis during a period of high drama. Increasingly lethal air defences encouraged both countries to escape the atmosphere altogether and deploy space-based imagery satellites. Today, orbital imagery is a fixture of intelligence, yet there are real concerns about the safety of satellites. Recent anti-satellite tests by China and Russia reinforced these fears. Stand-off intelligence platforms might offer a safe way of eliciting information that increases stability, but what counts as a safe distance remains unclear.

What do we make from this curious history? Intelligence contests might reduce the risk of war by providing information that reduces insecurity, and by providing non-military options for states in competition. Sometimes states seem to act according to this logic, letting intelligence contests play out according to tacit rules of the game, and quietly accepting covert action as an alternative to military force. At other times, however, states are often infuriated by espionage and covert action, and spy scares lead states closer to conflict. The evolution of imagery suggests that technology alone cannot account for this shifting attitude towards intelligence.

This is not to say that technology is irrelevant; states pay close attention to new innovations and spend a lot of time and money devising counter-measures. The nature of their response, however, probably depends on deeper political factors. High-tech spying is tolerable when underlying relations are dull and predictable, and when states are content to let intelligence agencies monitor the peace. But when relations sour, states are likely to fear the worst. In these cases, they are more likely to view foreign espionage as a prelude to hostile action. Even distant technical collection activities look sinister in a crisis. Intelligence activities do not cause political conflicts, but they might exacerbate existing tensions.

This logic might tell us something about cyberspace competition. Some have warned that the domain's peculiar technological characteristics make digital spying a dangerous business. The reason is that cyberspace espionage and sabotage use the same methods. From the defender's perspective, it is impossible to tell whether an intrusion is simply designed to steal information, or whether it is a prelude to a damaging attack. The result is a 'cybersecurity dilemma' that increases the chances of conflict. Escalation by miscalculation is more likely, according to this logic, when it is impossible to tell the difference between normal intelligence gathering and preparations for offensive action.

Yet cyberspying has been a fact of great power politics for decades, and there is no evidence that it has led to great power crises. The United States and China routinely accuse one another of large-scale espionage, for example, but this has not led to crises or military escalation. Instead, their cyberspace activities appear to be part of a long-running intelligence contest rather than a test of raw power. Intelligence contests are competitions in which great powers fight over information rather than military dominance. Indeed, they can be a release valve when great powers are locked in competition but prefer to avoid conflict. Rather than foreshadowing violence, aggressive cyberspace espionage might suggest a durable cold war.

Aggressive collection could be dangerous in a crisis in which adversaries are mobilising for possible military action. In such a case, leaders might view revelations of cyberspace espionage as evidence that their

enemies are preparing for war. They might reasonably fear losing important tactical information, or, in the worst case, losing control of their own
communications. This is certainly plausible, and leaders seeking peaceful off-ramps from dangerous crises would be wise to take the danger into
account. But again, the factors leading to instability in war are more political than technical. Misperception can occur in a number of ways in a
crisis because leaders are deeply mistrustful of one another, by definition.
They might misunderstand the purpose of military movements or mis-
construe diplomatic rhetoric. Fractured and unstable political relations,
not technology, are the underlying cause of trouble.

The relationship between diplomacy and intelligence is akin to the
relationship between diplomacy and force. Scholars have long debated
whether certain military technologies are inherently destabilising.
According to this logic, the deployment of offensive weapons makes war
likely because it makes conquest easy. Insecurity abounds when the
offence is dominant, increasing the risk of arms racing and military conflict. Similarly, some have warned about highly complex militaries relying on elaborate coordination schemes. Technology and bureaucracy
conspire to encourage risky behaviour because leaders need to move
quickly, or their military forces will be disorganised and vulnerable to
attack.

Others have challenged these claims. The same weapon system might
appear to different observers as offensive or defensive. Much depends on
their view of the adversary's intentions. If observers believe that their
adversaries are bloody-minded and risk-acceptant, they are more likely
to view weapons as offensive. If they believe their adversaries are inse-
cure and cautious, however, they will view the same weapons as less
threatening. Technology matters on the battlefield, but the political
implications depend on perceptions of international politics. Stable relations, even if unfriendly, will predispose leaders to view enemy technologies as relatively unthreatening. Unstable relations will cause them to
assume the opposite.

The same might be true for intelligence. I say 'might' because this is
very much an open question among researchers, and there are plenty of
other candidate hypotheses about intelligence and war. But if this intui-
tion is correct, then the implication is straightforward: intelligence is neither a force for peace nor a cause of conflict. Sometimes intelligence
agencies can reinforce stability by revealing information that reduces

misunderstandings. Rival states may coexist peacefully, letting their secret services battle for information rather than letting their militaries prepare for battle. In these cases, intelligence not only reduces the risk of war by clarifying the balance of power, it also provides a way for states to compete without risking too much. In other cases, however, espionage can make conflict more likely by aggravating mutual hostility and mistrust. When relations are particularly nasty, states may be convinced that their rivals are bent on political agitation and regime change. Under these conditions the discovery of espionage efforts will look ominous and threatening, especially if intelligence chiefs are amateurs and their agencies are bureaucratically immature. Ham-fisted collection may be indistinguishable from attempted subversion, reinforcing everyone's worst fears and creating powerful incentives to prepare for war.

All of this rests on the nature of state rivalries at any given time. Secret intelligence is a peculiar business, to be sure, but it is ultimately a tool of statecraft. How leaders use this tool, and how others respond, depends on their policy goals and strategic beliefs. In this sense, intelligence contests reflect and amplify international relations. Understanding the effects of spying will depend on grasping the politics behind the spies.

Carl Benz with his wife Bertha in a Benz Viktoria,
his first car with four wheels, 1893.

THE GERMANS AND THEIR CARS: HISTORY OF A LOVE AFFAIR

Katja Hoyer

he internal combustion engine is a beautiful thing. It has brought life to machines. For millennia, man-made constructions were propelled forward by external forces – coaches were drawn by horses, ships blown by the wind, farm machinery pulled by oxen, mills turned through the force of water. Machines of any description were passive recipients of energy, lifeless once the external source of their movement was removed. The internal combustion engine changed that. Turning fuel into kinetic energy through controlled explosions, it propels vehicles from within, making them independent organisms. It was the engine that made the car an almost lifelike creation, revolutionising and personalising our relationship with transport.

The electrification of movement will be yet another revolution; it removes the combustion engine – the beating, messy, physical heart of the car – and replaces it with the still, clean, chemical energy of batteries. This is more than a pragmatic adjustment. It will change the bond between man and machine forever.

When the German engineer Carl Benz designed his Patent-Motorwagen in 1885 he could not have known what a milestone it would be in the history of mankind. He had long been working on fuel-powered engines but this was the first time he had installed one in a vehicle that could move people around independently. His wife, Bertha Benz, whose dowry had financed the project, proved remaining sceptics wrong by taking her two teenage sons on a 66-mile trip from the city of Mannheim to her home town of Pforzheim in the Patent-Motorwagen. The Benzes had done it: personal travel in a self-propelled machine had become a reality. Today, more than one billion cars drive along the roads of the world, yet not much has changed from the basic principle: a fuel-powered engine turns a number of wheels, and, sitting on the seats attached to them, the passengers move forward.

Of course, there is still much argument among Europeans about who invented the first car, but Germans like to think it was their Carl Benz. His name and those of other early pioneers, such as Wilhelm Maybach and Gottlieb Daimler, who all began to use combustion engines in the mid-1880s, have retained their evocative ring through nearly a century and a half of motoring history. When they set out to build the first ever cars, Germany itself had barely begun to exist as a state. The country's young Kaiser Wilhelm II reflected the zeitgeist, and his Emperor's Prize of 1907 was a precursor to the German Grand Prix.

As the country stumbled through its troubled history in the twentieth century, the car drove both progress and destruction. Adolf Hitler was arguably the first German politician who understood the emotive power of the car and tried to exploit this for his own ends. He built the country's famed motorways in the 1930s which, as work creation schemes, became an important tool in the longing for pride and dignity experienced by a nation that had lost a war. The resulting autobahn system survived defeat, bombing and the taint cast over it by its ideological origins. Today, 70% of its network is free of any speed restrictions, and that means so much more to Germans than just being able to drive fast. The freedom and pride in automotive engineering it evokes are a part of the national psyche – the reason it has survived generations of politicians arguing for a speed limit, wielding accident figures and environmental concerns.

Hitler left Germany with another, equally enduring car legacy. He ordered the engineer and car designer Ferdinand Porsche to create a vehicle for the masses, a true people's car, a *Volkswagen*. While the war got in the way of delivering the clever design, the idea endured, and it appealed to the British victors after 1945. Both VW itself, as well as Hitler's brand new *Autostadt* (car city), Wolfsburg, survived. The VW Beetle became a symbol of the miraculous West German economic recovery and Wolfsburg still houses the world's largest car plant. West Germans and their occupiers understood the importance of the car to German economic and psychological recovery and facilitated a spectacular comeback on both fronts.

But the car is not just psychologically intrinsic to Germanness. The industry is also an integral part of the country's economic nervous system, currently worth 378.2 billion euros and employing more than 800,000 people, the single biggest sector of Europe's largest economy. Much of this hinges on the combustion engine and the hundreds of its attendant parts and processes. Over 300,000 people work in parts production and delivery. While much of the industry has been outsourced to other countries over the years, all parts of the chain of car production still have a huge stake in Germany.

We are now on the brink of an equally important stage in the development of German car production, though, with the transition to electrification. Politicians and industry leaders are understandably worried. In Germany alone, the move to electric vehicles could cost more than 400,000 jobs by 2030. But as the sector scrambles to make this transition work, it also sees it as an opportunity. Porsche, one of Germany's most prestigious car makers, has taken a huge stake in the Croatian company Rimac, which specialises in high-performance components for electro-mobility. Together, they say, they want to write a new chapter in the history of the automotive industry.

But will a fully electric German car industry lack a heart? Ed Conway, economist, historian and economics editor of Sky News in the UK, explains that electric motors and car parts are important but 'really, it's all about the battery; that's where 40–60% of the value of a car will be.' European countries are throwing enormous sums of money at the issue. So-called gigafactories, which will produce car batteries, are being built, such as Tesla's Giga Berlin, and they will bring jobs too. But this is only one part of the chain. Europe currently imports the necessary raw materials as well as the intricate chemical engineering. 'Competing with China in this regard will be difficult,' says Conway. 'It's comparable to the Industrial Revolution, where we in Europe invented the car before the technology was exported to the rest of the world. We had a head start. The same is true for battery technology in Asia, where Japan, China and Korea have long worked on chemical engineering while we remained protective of our traditional industry here.' Ray Massey, motoring editor for the *Daily Mail*, agrees: 'Germans have always been good at intricate physical engineering – cars, machinery, toys. It's something they have been very protective about.'

There is some hope that the vast amounts of investment in new technologies will go some way to transforming the industry successfully, while retaining its heritage and tradition. Volkswagen doubled its profit from battery-powered cars in 2021 and beat Tesla in Europe with a market share of 26%. But the size and range of Volkswagen hides the fact that on individual electric car models, Tesla's Model 3 outdid all its contemporary German rivals in Germany.

The EU has imposed ambitious targets on the whole sector in an effort to force a shift towards electric vehicles. Brussels wants nothing less than the death of the internal combustion engine by 2035. It has proposed cutting CO_2 emissions from cars by 55% between 2021 and 2030. By 2035, it wants to raise the bar to 100%, making it impossible for car manufacturers to sell vehicles with fossil fuel-powered engines anywhere within the European Union. If this road map becomes a legal reality, the industry has just over a decade to adapt more than a century's worth of tradition.

On the whole, the German automotive industry has accepted the challenge. Its leaders agree that climate change is a global problem that needs to be addressed as a matter of urgency. The transport sector accounts for one-fifth of global carbon dioxide emissions. So there are good reasons to cut down on the amount of environmental damage caused by cars. In addition, there are concerns about air quality in urban areas. When travel was temporarily reduced during the lockdowns of the Covid pandemic in 2020, London and Paris reported drops of up to 70% in the levels of toxic nitrogen oxides in the air. Fully electrified traffic in urban areas could do wonders for air quality within a matter of weeks.

The new German government is also keen to modernise. The coalition contains a buoyant Green party which has taken key cabinet positions, such as the economics ministry, now headed by Robert Habeck, former leader of the Greens. In a controversial move, former Greenpeace boss Jennifer Morgan has been appointed Germany's climate envoy, an indication of the extent to which activism has been reeled into the country's politics. It is therefore no surprise that the coalition's programme for the next four years pledges support for 'the transformation of the automobile sector in order to achieve climate targets'. The government intends to make Germany 'the leading market for electromobility'. By 2030, it wants at least 15 million fully electric vehicles on the road, although only 500,000 new battery-powered cars were sold last year, 13% of new registrations. But the trend is rising. The 2021 figures mark an increase of more than 300% compared to the previous year – no wonder, as government incentives to switch are considerable. Germans can get up to 9,000 euros to subsidise the purchase of a new electric vehicle, which is often enough to convince the sceptics. Surveys from 2019, when the bonus was introduced, show that around half of Germans were considering an electric or hybrid vehicle the next time they bought a car.

Given the rapid increase in sales of electric vehicles, it is tempting to assume that this trend will continue. But there are indications already that public support for electrification is beginning to plateau. Surveys suggest the willingness to buy an electric car has dropped below the half-way mark. Four in five Germans engage in extended online research before they buy a car, a process that seems to have taken the shine off the technology. A recent study by the research group Deutsche Automobil Treuhand (DAT) found that, ironically, it was the promise of immense state subsidies for electric vehicles in 2019 that led to increased research activity on them which, in turn, cranked up scepticism. Germans began to wonder whether the sourcing of raw materials and electricity is really more environmentally friendly than fossil fuels. But the biggest concern, quoted by 79% of respondents, was what would happen to their battery after use. As the excitement around the new technology is giving way to cold analysis, an increasing number of Germans have turned away from electric vehicles and it looks as if they will have to be brought back through legislation rather than argument.

And therein lies the industry's problem. The decision against a petrol or diesel car is almost always driven by rational argument and research, not impulse or emotion. For many Germans, cars are much more than a means of transport. The DAT's report found that well over half of Germans experience a sense of happiness just looking at their car, an emotion unlikely to be triggered by a glance at the AEG washing machine. Four out of five said they see driving as a 'fun' thing to do, not the typical reaction when the Siemens vacuum cleaner comes out of the cupboard. Around 20% of German car owners even admitted they regularly take their car out for a drive just for the sheer joy of it. Enjoyment is not something Bosch needs to factor in when designing electric screwdrivers.

It is hard for Germans to love an electric vehicle in the same intense way. Electrics are quiet; they don't roar, splutter or growl. They smell clean and neutral without the sharp whiff of petrol, oil, lubricants and exhaust fumes. They just seem less physical. Their batteries operate on complicated and invisible chemical processes, which power a relatively simple motor with much fewer parts. It is hard to look at the straightfor-ward mechanics that propel an electric car and feel the same fascination that many experience when looking at the intricate levers, cogs and pistons that move conventional cars.

At the higher end of the market, car makers who rely on the emotional connection between man and machine to sell their cars have been rightly concerned about severing links with the combustion engine. Italian car producers Ferrari and Lamborghini have lobbied their government hard to push back against Brussels' plans. As a result, Roberto Cingolani, Italy's minister for ecological transition, is seeking an exemption to allow both brands to continue to sell high-performance engines, particularly their evocative V12 units. Former Lamborghini engineer Maurizio Reggiani has noted: 'I believe that what we sell is emotion, and part of that emotion comes from the sound of the engine. It's the sound Lamborghini customers want to hear.' Some German car manufacturers agree. Oliver Zipse, chief executive of BMW and president of the European Automobile Manufacturers' Association, has also argued that 'For very small manufacturers who, in the bigger picture of overall emissions play almost no role, there are good arguments for considering these exemptions.'

Volkswagen chief executive Herbert Diess, on the other hand, is less worried about the transition to electric vehicles. While he is keen to manage the process carefully, he feels that concerns over the loss of the entire industry have been 'overstated'. After all, this is not just about the engine, he argues. 'A lot of the car remains the same; it's still seats, paint, body work, interiors, wheels, axles.'

The sector needs to look at more than just current sales figures, job retention and whether it can still sell the skin and bones of a German car if it contains a Chinese heart. Working in an American or Chinese battery factory on German soil does not replace the heritage of a chain that ranges from the very first idea, through the engineering process to assembly. German car making is nearly as old as the nation itself and embedded in its heart, soul and mind. If vast sums of money are being invested to adapt the country's motoring heritage to modern realities and sensibilities, they need to be invested with an eye on history as well as the economy.

The entire relationship of the nation to its cars will change with electrification. Replacing combustion engines with batteries is not a like-for-like swap. The decision to transform century-old industrial traditions within the course of a decade is currently a top-down process rather than the result of entrepreneurial evolution. Instead of being whipped through by target-driven bureaucrats, this process should be a careful one, given due thought and public discussion. We are about to give up one of man's most emotive mechanical creations; more is at stake than facts and figures.

Sean Connery as James Bond in
You Only Live Twice, 1967.

BOND OR BLOFELD: WAR, ESPIONAGE AND SECRECY IN THE TWENTY-FIRST CENTURY

Richard J. Aldrich and Christopher Moran

In 2009, a fascinating essay appeared on James Bond. Titled 'The Spy Who Loved Globalization', it was penned by David Earnest and James Rosenau, two top experts on international relations, who explored the connections between real-world security threats and spy fiction. They observed that as early as the 1960s, Ian Fleming, author of the James Bond novels, had anticipated the messy post-Cold War world. Although Fleming's first novels, such as *Casino Royale*, focused on chasing Russian spies, quite quickly his attention shifted and 007 was wrestling with global miscreants, ungoverned spaces and sprawling 'new wars'. His Bond villains anticipated the bad boys of globalisation: part terrorist, part international financier, part global criminal and part spy. Remarkably, decades before political scientists debated these sorts of ideas, Fleming had begun to forecast our future enemies.

Today, the resonance of recent war and espionage with the world of 007 looks even stronger. In past decades, professional spies rather sniffily dismissed Bond movies as mere action thrillers that had little to do with the real world of patient intelligence collection and analysis. Richard Moore, the current head of MI6, recently showed his ambivalence to the franchise with the Twitter hashtag '#ForgetJamesBond'. However, changes in the nature of conflict, often associated with globalisation, terror and the internet, have not only reshaped our enemies but are also changing the intelligence and security agencies that seek to guard us. A 'war on terror' that has lasted 20 years, together with two long conflicts in Afghanistan and Iraq, have radically transformed our spies. All around the world, the boundary between espionage, special operations and online warfare has blurred, giving rise to a new typology that some have dubbed the 'soldier-spy'. But are today's secret operatives emulating James Bond, or his menacing enemy Ernst Blofeld?

One thing is clear: the new soldier-spy is barely hidden. Militarised and pumped up by vast spending on the war on terror, intelligence agencies have become much bigger and also noisier as they surge towards war zones, most recently Syria, Libya, Yemen and Ukraine. The Western intelligence community now boasts a budget of almost $100 billion a year and more than a million Americans have top secret clearances. As we have observed elsewhere, together with the fact that information is every-where, this also means lots of leaks, and so what was hush-hush on a Tuesday is often on the front page of the *Washington Post* on Thursday. Secrecy is in short supply, and agencies that once worked in the shadows are increasingly in the spotlight.

Secrecy, even more than intelligence, has long been a form of state power. So, while states have vastly inflated what some have called the 'covert sphere', full of espionage and special activities, this has inevitably made them more visible. If spies and special forces are everywhere, it is hardly surprising that they are also on the front pages of our newspapers. Yet leaders hate this decline of secrecy, especially when they are not con-trolling it. Under Barack Obama, the war on 'national security leakers' took on a ferocious intensity, with a record number of prosecutions. Biden reportedly shares this obsessive desire to protect secrets and is still in pursuit of Edward Snowden and Julian Assange. Britain is about to intro-duce a new Official Secrets Act designed to crack down on leakers. Remarkably, in December 2021, Denmark secretly detained one of its most distinguished intelligence chiefs, Lars Findsen, reportedly for talk-ing to the press about internet interception.

Snowden's famous revelations, made in the summer of 2013, seemed to focus on threats to citizen privacy. In fact, the most dramatic change these disclosures illuminated was the decline of government secrecy, especially around national security. While the ethics of whistle-blowing have been much debated, few have attempted to explain the dynamics of this grow-ing climate of exposure. The changing nature of intelligence work, which is increasingly merging with big data and open source, is partly responsi-ble for this. But there is also cultural change, since many intelligence contractors – such as Snowden – are at best agnostic about the national security state. The decline of secrecy has presented national security chiefs with one of their biggest future challenges since they have no choice but to embrace new technology, yet many technologists are fundamen-tally 'Californian' in outlook and believe that information should be free.

Spy chiefs are fighting back. Unable to control the torrent of revela-tions about secret things, they have instead tried to shape it with public

affairs. Every morning, on the seventh floor of the CIA's main building at
its leafy campus at Langley, Virginia, the director meets with key managers. Much of their time is devoted to what was said about them in the
media the previous day. At first glance this seems like institutional vanity,
but in fact it reflects a hard reality. Like it or not, the CIA is not just an
intelligence agency, it is increasingly symbolic of wider debates in
American foreign policy. Whether the issues are about interventionism
versus isolationism, presidential versus democratic control of foreign policy, or core values versus national security imperatives, the CIA is often
in the centre of a very public stage. Its recent trajectory is highly contested, and the arguments over signature strikes, torture and secret pris-
ons, which have raged for nearly two decades, are only some examples.
In this climate, the CIA has never been more anxious to sculpt its own
image.

The directors of the CIA do this as top managers, and also in retirement. For more than 50 years, much of our knowledge about the agency
has come from memoirs, often written by its former leaders. JFK's legend-
ary spy chief, Allen Dulles, was the first; frustrated by the way the Bay of
Pigs hastened the end of his career, he resolved to publish a book defending his profession. As Jules Gaspard has observed, since 9/11, CIA chiefs
have increasingly turned to writing to complete in public the unfinished
business that privately dogged them during their careers. Former directors now team up with CIA publicists as ghostwriters to produce memoirs
that are widely read and influential. Published in 2007, George Tenet's
memoir of his time in the Bush administration, *At the Center of the Storm*,
was only beaten to the top slot in the bestseller lists by the seventh and
final volume of the *Harry Potter* series.

The 2012 film *Zero Dark Thirty* underlines the manner in which both the
CIA and Obama used Hollywood to embrace a new kind of secrecy. This
film had multiple purposes: it celebrated the militarisation of the CIA
and the fusion of its espionage activity with special forces, while also
seeking to defend the role of torture. The film was boosted by the CIA's
public affairs office, which wanted to evoke the spirit of James Bond.
Indeed, federal assistance to *Zero Dark Thirty* was so substantial that it
stirred political controversy, and so the release of the film had to be
delayed until after the presidential election. Remarkably, in 2013, *Zero
Dark Thirty* missed the Oscar for Best Picture only because it was beaten
by another CIA-assisted covert action film called *Argo*, about the rescue

of hostages from Iran in 1979. The Oscars were announced by Michelle Obama from the West Wing of the White House. Secret activities had never been more un-secret or spectacular.

Zero Dark Thirty celebrated the CIA's warrior tradition. In 2008, Michael Hayden, America's most experienced intelligence chief, observed that the agency had begun to resemble its historical predecessor, the Office of Strategic Services, a commando unit created by First World War veteran General 'Wild Bill' Donovan that gloried in special operations. In 2011, when the softly spoken Leon Panetta, former head of the Office of the Management of the Budget, took over as director of the CIA, he expected to be managing a rather actuarial intelligence organisation focused on analysis. To his surprise, he soon realised that he was now 'the combatant commander in the war on terrorism'.

This transformation was not just about the CIA, but instead about the wider nature of war itself. It extended to new ways in which battles were being fought in Afghanistan and Iraq. While the CIA had been busy embracing more war-fighting, the cutting-edge fighters of US special forces had borrowed the techniques of the CIA. The war on terror has transformed Special Operations Command (SOCOM). Driven by the ferocious challenge of suicide bombers in Baghdad and Basra, they had fused technical exploitation of seized computers and mobile phones with geolocation and midnight kill squads. Science was allowing the application of national resources to tactical events in real time. With a new global mandate, SOCOM has almost tripled in size since 9/11, commanding around 100,000 personnel. Presidents love US special forces, which now have a presence in over 100 countries; more importantly, their new approach to war is being emulated around the world.

Covert action is the shop window for a new kind of warfare. For generations, scholars have defined covert action as plausibly deniable interventions, so the sponsor's hand is neither apparent nor acknowledged. But changes in technology and the media, combined with the rise of special forces and private military companies, mean that today we are entering a grey zone of ambiguous warfare or hybrid war. We are witnessing the rise of a remarkable new phenomenon that Rory Cormac has called 'implausible deniability'. This does not mean the end of covert action. Instead, leaders are embracing a curious kind of performative secrecy and exploiting the fear that it creates to drive a new kind of interventionism.

Conventional wisdom suggests that states engage in covert action when they can plausibly deny sponsorship. The execution of the act itself may not necessarily be secret – assassinations are an all too visible example – but the authorship should be hidden both during and afterwards. To do these deeds, states must be able to deny involvement, and in a believable manner. This has created a conceptually neat but flawed understanding of covert action. In fact, many historic covert actions were an open secret: implausibly deniable. The CIA's failed attempt to overthrow Fidel Castro at the Bay of Pigs in 1961, together with large-scale paramilitary operations in Laos, Angola and Afghanistan, are examples where denials lacked plausibility. More recently, the Kremlin initially denied intervention in Ukraine in 2014 and still denies interference in the 2016 US presidential election. These denials were obviously false, yet these operations did not fall outside the boundaries of covert action, nor were they failures.

In reality, a spectrum of attribution now exists, since covert action has multiple audiences, both internal and external. Plausible deniability has long been flimsy, especially regarding paramilitary operations. This is even more the case today with the collapse of secrecy triggered by the proliferation of electronic whistle-blowing. Implausible deniability is also linked to the growth of special forces and private military actors, which have further increased the grey space between secrecy and visibility. Yet implausible deniability does not spell the end of covert action. Increasingly, political leaders wish to have their cake and eat it, avoiding constitutional accountability for risky operations while harnessing the benefits of open secrecy. Implausible deniability allows them to frighten enemies, exploit ambiguity and even 'hang tough' by boasting about deploying spies and special forces.

But as world leaders embrace their performative spies, do they love the dashing James Bond, or do they prefer Ernst Blofeld? The 2008 death of former FSB officer Alexander Litvinenko and the 2018 poisoning of former Russian GRU operative Sergei Skripal both point to a new and darker form of public covert action, designed as a deterrent to others who contemplate defection or disobedience. Putin's love of visible revenge in the face of diplomatic reprisals and significant economic sanctions makes him important as a trendsetter in grey warfare. Michael Goodman and David Gioe have argued that because we have tended to view secret services as 'secret', there is a lack of ideas about overt intelligence-driven attacks as a form of strategic messaging.

Russia has led the way with theatrical murder, but others are rushing to catch up. An increasing number of states carry out assassinations. In October 2018, Jamal Khashoggi, a journalist working for the *Washington Post*, entered the Saudi consulate in Istanbul and promptly disappeared. He was brutally murdered inside the building by a killer squad of 15, flown in specially by the Saudi regime. Months later, Gina Haspel, the director of the CIA, visited Turkey and listened to chilling audio recordings from bugs inside the Saudi consulate where the body was cut up by an operative wearing headphones and listening to music. Espionage has often been dark, but this was beyond anything imagined by Blofeld and was closer to *Reservoir Dogs*.

As with Putin, the denials were deliberately laughable. There can be no doubt that this was an orchestrated Saudi intelligence operation planned long in advance. Only a few hours after Khashoggi's murder in Istanbul, Saudi internet trolls launched a coordinated propaganda campaign designed to frame him as a terrorist and a secret intelligence operative of Turkey. They even suggested the narrative of his disappearance was an internet fabrication by enemies of Riyadh. This bizarre campaign also focused on his fiancée, Hatice Cengiz, alleging that she was a spy. Donald Trump did his best to dismiss the affair, while brazenly prioritising American arms sales.

In early 2020, Trump went further and ordered the strikes on General Soleimani and Mohsen Fakhrizadeh, two Iranian special forces luminaries, with CIA drones, sparking a new round of debates about government assassination. Months later, the Israelis joined in with robot machine guns. The death of Fakhrizadeh, a nuclear scientist, was not especially surprising since half a dozen of Teheran's top technicians have been killed and injured since 2007. The notable thing about this attack, though, was the use of an artificial intelligence-assisted, remote-controlled machine gun aimed from a fake broken-down pick-up truck. All these episodes straddle the boundary between espionage, special forces and dark science. While public affairs departments have rushed to romanticise 'Wild Bill' Donovan and the warrior tradition, their critics have pointed to the use of technology for disinformation, interrogation or remote death. The warrior is ultimately about courage on the battlefield, but the Tuesday morning 'kill list' rather smacks of cowardly bureaucrats pushing buttons.

In the twenty-first century, war and espionage are changing fast because familiar boundaries are being ripped up. These include the barriers between spies and special forces, openness and secrecy, even public and private. Compared to the days before 9/11, the legal, political and technological infrastructures that now sustain our global 'remote wars' are almost unrecognisable. It is a matter of style as well as substance. More than ten countries have conducted deadly drone strikes, and twice that number of countries now have the capability. Robots and poisons are all the rage. Maybe James Bond was emblematic of yesterday's spies, but Ernst Blofeld is the face of the future.

ATTEMPT TO ASSASSINATE THE EMPEROR OF THE FRENCH (THE ORSINI PLOT).

Illustration depicting the attempted
assassination of Emperor Napoleon III.
George Barnett Smith, ca. 1890.

KEEPING IT SIMPLE: HOW TECHNOLOGY SHAPES THE TERROR THREAT

Suzanne Raine

In late 1857, the Italian nationalist Felice Orsini visited England and asked a Birmingham-based engineer called Joseph Taylor to manufacture six copies of a bomb he had designed. The bomb used fulminate of mercury and was designed to explode on impact.

Orsini tested the bomb in Sheffield and Devon with the aid of Simon Bernard, a French radical. Once they knew it worked, Orsini travelled to Paris, intending to kill Emperor Napoleon III. On the evening of 14 January 1858, Orsini and his accomplices threw three bombs at the carriage carrying the emperor and his wife. They were unharmed, but eight people were killed and 156 wounded; Orsini was executed by guillotine two months later. There followed a brief swelling of anti-British sentiment in France because the bombs had been made and tested in Britain.

What became known as the Orsini bomb was an important step in the development of terrorist capabilities. It was a percussion-triggered, shrapnel-scattering IED and became synonymous with terrorism and insurgency even after the invention of dynamite in 1866. Among others, Orsini bombs were used by Garibaldi in Italy in the 1860s and the Paris Communards in 1871; they were thrown at Isma'il Pasha, the Khedive of Egypt, in 1866, killed at least 30 in Barcelona in 1893, and in 1908 were used by anti-colonial insurgents in an attempt to derail a train in Calcutta. There were elements of Orsini's design in the bomb which killed Tsar Alexander II.

Critical to the Orsini bomb's success was not only how effective it was, but how easy it was to operate. It was easy to get the component parts, it was easy to construct and use, it worked well enough, and it could be carried in your pocket. The technique was an enabler; it could challenge the state monopoly on violence. Karl Heinzen, the German revolutionary, had argued in 1853 that radicals needed to 'devise some sort of missile which one man can throw into a group of a few hundred, killing them all', which would give 'a few lone individuals the terrifying power to threaten the safety of whole masses of barbarians'. Now they had it.

Creativity and invention have always been the key elements of a successful terrorist attack. There is no clear correlation between cost and effectiveness, or between complexity and effectiveness. The cheapest and simplest attacks can be just as deadly as those which take time, expertise and money. That was demonstrated, for example, by the attack in Nice on Bastille Day 2016, when a 19-tonne truck was driven into the crowds, killing 86 and wounding 450. It could also be argued that 9/11, the most audacious terrorist attack of all, was devastatingly simple in technical terms.

As new technology developed throughout the twentieth century, terrorists tested how it might be useful to them. Evolving technology consistently introduces new possibilities for both attacker and defender. The more inventive terrorists became, the more defensive measures needed to be put in place. As new countermeasures were introduced, terrorists became increasingly inventive to evade them. The development of defensive measures needed to avoid becoming draconian and paranoid, but also to be as imaginative as the terrorists, particularly since the damning conclusion that the failure to prevent 9/11 had been down to a 'failure of imagination'. Alongside this escalatory technical competition, there was also a rush to block access to *materiel*, or enable it to be better tracked, or to introduce comprehensive surveillance capabilities such as CCTV. Thus, in part the story of terrorism since the Orsini bomb has been a race of invention and counter-invention, a race to identify and plug vulnerabilities.

Hijacking has been a tactic since planes first came into regular use; the first recorded hijack took place in 1931 in Peru, when armed revolutionaries approached the pilot on the ground and demanded, unsuccessfully, to be flown to their destination. The first in-air hijack is said to have been in 1942, when two New Zealanders, a South African and a British man overpowered their captors in an Italian seaplane which was taking them to a prisoner-of-war camp. Hijacking of commercial airliners for political reasons grew in the 1940s and 50s, but really took off in the 60s and 70s. As this danger became clear, the US Federal Aviation Administration (FAA) issued a directive in 1961 which prohibited unauthorised personnel from carrying concealed firearms and interfering with the crew. From 1968 to 1972, there were 326 hijackings, mostly in the United States, and this obviously prompted action. In 1970, President Nixon introduced a directive to promote security at airports and electronic surveillance, and in 1972 the FAA issued emergency rules requiring all passengers and their carry-on baggage to be screened. These measures came into effect in 1973, and most of the architecture of modern airports – X-ray machines and walk-through detectors – was installed. Hijackers of the 1970s went to increasingly elaborate lengths to evade X-ray machines, although this sometimes just involved going around rather than through them. The hijackers of the Air France Airbus in 1976 which landed in Entebbe boarded during a stopover in Athens, where there had been no strict control of passengers in transit from other aircraft.

As hijacking became harder, terrorists turned to blowing up the aircraft instead. Pan Am flight 103 from Frankfurt to Detroit via New York was blown up over Lockerbie in Scotland by a bomb on-board, killing all 243 passengers and 16 crew and 11 local residents on the ground in December 1988. The Semtex bomb was believed to have been hidden inside a Toshiba radio cassette player, inside a Samsonite suitcase, and detonated by a barometric sensor triggered by altitude. Semtex is a plastic explosive first manufactured in Czechoslovakia in the late 1950s for military use and commercial blasting, but it was widely exported and was soon favoured by Iranian- and Libyan-sponsored terrorist organisations, as well as the IRA, because it was plastic and odourless and difficult to detect. It became closely associated with terrorist attacks, and rules governing its exportation were progressively tightened. But the critical change was a simple scientific one: in the 1990s, a detection taggant was added which gave Semtex a scent, producing a distinctive vapour signature. Batches of Semtex made before 1990, however, are still untagged, although it is not known how much of this untagged Semtex still exists. The manufacturer states that even this untagged Semtex can now be detected.

The ban on liquids and the requirement for laptops and other electronic items to be screened separately were again a response to the development by terrorists of new techniques to evade screening. In 2006, the British-Pakistani Rashid Rauf devised what has become known as the 'liquid bomb plot', planning to use concentrated hydrogen peroxide in ordinary sports drinks bottles to blow up flights from Heathrow to the US and Canada. Rauf's analysis had been that it was very difficult for airport security measures to detect liquid explosives. The plot was detected before he had a chance to try it. The lasting legacy is that all liquids taken on to flights must be 100ml or less and contained in a single, one-litre capacity transparent bag, measuring 20cm by 20cm. This bag must be sealed and placed in the security tray, separately from the cabin bag. Similarly, the requirement for electronics larger than a mobile phone to be screened separately stems from the discovery in 2017 that terrorists had developed a new concealment method.

On 27 October 2010, a woman dropped off two packages at the FedEx and UPS offices in Sana'a, Yemen, to be sent to addresses in Chicago. Inside were Hewlett-Packard Laserjet printers packed with explosives. The Saudi Minister of Interior, Muhammad bin Nayef, provided the US and UK with tracking numbers of the parcels. One was intercepted in Dubai, and the other at East Midlands airport. In the UK, the printer was subjected to explosives tests, sniffer dogs, X-rays and chemical swabs, and no explosives were detected. They concluded that there was no bomb in the printer. But reports from Dubai made them look again. It had been so hard to find because of the sophistication of the concealment inside the toner cartridge, and the fact that the cartridges were filled with penta-erythritol tetranitrate (PETN), an odourless military-grade white pow-der plastic explosive, of an extremely high concentration. The bombs had probably been made by Ibrahim al-Assiri, master bomb-maker of Al-Qaeda in the Arabian Peninsula (AQAP). They would be triggered by a mobile phone alarm, activated by the battery, which would send power through a filament and ignite an initiator, causing the PETN to detonate. The device was wired such that the printer would continue to work and the bomb would not show up in an X-ray. Al-Assiri experimented with the construction of non-metallic bombs, and is also thought to have made the bomb carried by Umar Farouk Abdulmutallab, a Nigerian who attempted to ignite chemical explosives sewn into his underwear on a plane between Amsterdam and Detroit on Christmas Day 2009.

These attacks were Al-Qaeda's closest aviation near misses since 9/11. In November 2010, AQAP published a detailed account of the planning for the printer cartridge attacks in their online magazine *Inspire*, the aim being to encourage others to conduct smaller but more frequent opera-tions 'to bleed the enemy to death'. The report gave the precise costs: two Nokia mobile phones, $150 each; two HP printers, $300 each; plus ship-ping, transport These incidents underline the difficulty created by the availability of everything, as exploited in AQAP's summer 2010 edition of

Inspire, which included an article titled 'Make a bomb in the Kitchen of your Mom'. Rather than stopping terrorists acquiring sophisticated capabilities, the challenge became to stop them acquiring everyday objects which might be used to deadly effect. Triacetone triperoxide (TATP) is a homemade explosive and presents, according to the FBI, a persistent threat to public safety because of readily available and inexpensive precursor materials, coupled with widely available instructions (the three chemical components are acetone, hydrogen peroxide and acid, all of which have legitimate uses). Salman Abedi, the man who attacked the Manchester Arena on 22 May 2017, killing 22, bought the components of his bomb online. His first attempt to get a friend to buy five litres of sulphuric acid from Amazon failed because the friend did not have the £76 it cost. The hydrogen peroxide was also purchased on Amazon – by his younger brother, using a debit card of a friend – at a cost of £185.92. Abedi apparently learned how to construct the bomb by watching videos on YouTube. The bomb was packed with nuts and bolts, all easily purchased. Given that the instructions on how to make TATP are so widely disseminated, and the ingredients are all dual-purpose, prevention has to focus on denial of access to those ingredients. One method is to raise understanding in order to help to identify abnormal purchase amounts. Another would be to increase the amount of unfocused surveillance; to use technology against technology. It might, in theory, be possible to set an algorithm to see everyone who buys quantities of ball bearings online, but it would require unprecedented collaboration between tech companies and the state, and would be classified as unacceptable intrusion.

Every aspect of Salman Abedi's planning was enabled by the internet. We assume he was radicalised at least in part online. He purchased the components, coordinated those purchases with friends, and researched the bomb-making techniques online. And the day after the attack, Daesh claimed responsibility online, crediting a 'soldier of the Caliphate'. Thus, the entire cycle of the relatively simple real-world attack was facilitated by technology. It enables terrorist groups to communicate, between each other and with the world. It is the vehicle for the proselytising recruitment myths, for publicising and claiming terrorist attacks, for building followers and glorifying deeds. Al-Qaeda's *Inspire* and Daesh's *Dabiq* magazine (now the weekly *Al-Naba*) would not exist were it not for the internet. Al-Qaeda were, in fact, early adopters of closed internet forums, where they built a followership and learned how to radicalise. To be a successful global franchise, it is important to be seen. Ayman al-Zawahiri, the leader of Al-Qaeda, has typically eschewed such newfangled outreach, and it has significantly reduced the impact of the brand. He is, however, as far as we know, still alive.

Access to the internet has become a dependency and a vulnerability: if terrorists are connecting then they can be seen, and can be caught. The effect of all-pervasive electronic surveillance is that they can no longer hold meetings in closed spaces, or use electronic communications. Daesh's media centre in Raqqa was flattened. If having a mobile phone means it is easier to find you, then don't carry one. Al-Qaeda learned the dangers of the satellite phone early on, and the lowly position of 'holder of the satellite phone' was not one the ambitious aspired to. When Afghanistan fell to the Taliban, President Biden suggested that 'over-the-horizon technology' would enable the US to continue countering terrorists. Maybe, but the effect of the technical arms race is to drive terrorists to simpler, improvised, non-technical options. The more technical the world becomes, the more the simple attack is most likely to succeed. The most effective terrorists operate without being detected, which means in this day and age that they need to go off-grid.

And what about the next generation of technologies? There will always be a trade-off between, on the one hand, the accessibility and deployability of technology and, on the other, its effect. Weapons of mass destruction have presented real challenges for terrorist groups because of the difficulty of acquisition and use or dispersal. Daesh experimented for five years in Syria and Iraq with drone swarms and the localised use of chemical weapons, and so has developed a battlefield capability. Drones can be bought easily online, although they can also be fitted with tracking technology. Analysts talk wearily about cyberterrorism, noting that it is difficult to see how to achieve a mass casualty effect. There is something naturally more alarming about the sci-fi-style attack than the low sophistication one, so the question is why the lure and fear of technology is not exploited more by terrorists. The answer may be prosaic: high-tech attacks are not yet as effective, or they are more vulnerable to detection.

CONTRIBUTORS

RICHARD ALDRICH is a Fellow of the Royal Historical Society, Professor of International Security at the University of Warwick and the author of many books including *GCHQ: The Uncensored Story of Britain's Most Secret Intelligence Agency* and *The Black Door: Spies, Secret Intelligence and British Prime Ministers.*

BRUCE ANDERSON is a British political columnist, currently working as a freelancer. Formerly a political editor at *The Spectator* and contributor to the *Daily Mail*, he wrote for *The Independent* from 2003 to 2010, and for *ConservativeHome* until 2012.

CLIVE ASLET is an award-winning architectural historian and journalist. During a long association with *Country Life*, he was editor for 13 years. As author of *The Edwardian Country House, The American Country House, Landmarks of Britain* and *Villages of Britain*, he is an authority on the countryside, British history and architecture, and life at the turn of the twentieth century on both sides of the Atlantic. A lifelong advocate of Classicism, he helped establish the Ax:son Johnson Centre for the Study of Classical Architecture at Cambridge in 2021.

DAVID J. BETZ is Reader in War Studies at King's College London, where he heads the Insurgency Research Group in the War Studies Department. He is a Senior Fellow at the Foreign Policy Research Institute and a consultant to the Development, Concepts and Doctrine Centre at the Ministry of Defence. He has written several books, including *Carnage and Connectivity: Landmarks in the Decline of Conventional Military Power.*

ANANYO BHATTACHARYA is a science writer based in London. His work has appeared in *The Economist*, *Nature* and elsewhere. Before journalism, he was a medical researcher at the Burnham Institute in San Diego, California. He holds a degree in physics from the University of Oxford and a PhD in protein crystallography from Imperial College London. His contribution to this collection is partly adapted from *The Man from the Future: The Visionary Life of John von Neumann*, his book on the legacy of Hungarian-American mathematician John von Neumann.

ELISABETH BRAW is a Resident Fellow at the American Enterprise Institute (AEI), where she focuses on defence and deterrence against Grey Zone threats. She is also a columnist with *Foreign Policy*, where she writes on national security and the globalised economy. Before joining AEI, Elisabeth was a Senior Research Fellow at the Royal United Services Institute, whose Modern Deterrence project she led. Prior to that, she worked at Control Risks, a global risk consultancy. Elisabeth is also a member of the steering committee of the Aurora Forum (the UK–Nordic–Baltic leader conference), a member of the UK National Preparedness Commission and an Associate Fellow at the European Leadership Network. Elisabeth started her career as a journalist, reporting for *Newsweek*, the *Christian Science Monitor* and the international *Metro* group of newspapers, among others. She regularly writes op-eds, including for the *Financial Times*, *Politico*, the *Frankfurter Allgemeine Zeitung* (writing in German) and the *Wall Street Journal*. She is also the author of *God's Spies: The Stasi's Cold War Espionage Campaign Inside the Church*, about the Stasi.

JIMENA CANALES is an expert in the nineteenth- and twentieth-century history of the physical sciences. She is the author of *Simply Einstein* and *Bedeviled: A Shadow History of Demons in Science*, and is currently a faculty member of the Graduate College at University of Illinois, Urbana-Champaign.

ARMAND D'ANGOUR is a Professor of Classics at the University of Oxford and Fellow of Jesus College, Oxford. He is the author of numerous articles and chapters on the literature and culture of ancient Greece and (as a former professional cellist) has conducted innovative research into reconstructing early Greek music. His books include *The Greeks and the New: Novelty in Ancient Greek Imagination and Experience*. His latest book *How to Innovate: An Ancient Guide to Creative Thinking* was published in 2021.

JOHN DARLINGTON is a professional archaeologist and Executive Director for World Monument's Fund Britain. He is the author of *Fake Heritage: Why We Rebuild Monuments*, a member of the Chartered Institute for Archaeologists and a Fellow of the Society of Antiquaries.

MARIA GOLIA, a long-time resident of Egypt, is the author of non-fiction books including *Photography and Egypt*, *Meteorite: Nature and Culture*, *Ornette Coleman: The Territory and the Adventure*, and *A Short History of Tomb-Raiding: The Epic Hunt for Egypt's Treasures*.

SAMUEL GREGG is Research Director at the Acton Institute. He has written and spoken extensively on questions of political economy, economic history, monetary theory and policy, and natural law theory. He is the author of 16 books, including *Wilhelm Röpke's Political Economy*; *Becoming Europe: Economic Decline, Culture, and How America Can Avoid a European Future* and *The Next American Economy: Nation, State and Markets in an Uncertain Age*. Two of his books have been short-listed for Conservative Book of the Year. Many of his books and over 400 articles and opinion pieces have been translated into a variety of languages. He also serves as a visiting scholar at the Feulner Institute of the Heritage Foundation.

KATJA HOYER is a German-British historian and journalist. She is a Visiting Research Fellow at King's College London and a Fellow of the Royal Historical Society. Katja writes for the *Washington Post*, *The Spectator*, *Die Welt* and other newspapers on current political affairs in Germany and Europe. She is the author of the bestselling *Blood and Iron: The Rise and Fall of the German Empire, 1871–1918*.

TIM JENKINS retired from the University of Cambridge, where he taught anthropology and religion, in October 2019. Since then, he has been writing a book on reports of flying saucer sightings, with the provisional title

Images of Elsewhere, which is near completion. Previous publications include *Religion in English Everyday Life*, *The Life of Property: House, Family and Inheritance in Béarn, South-West France*, and *Of Flying Saucers and Social Scientists: A Re-Reading of When Prophecy Fails and of Cognitive Dissonance*. He lives in Cambridge.

ANDREW KEEN is a commentator on the social impact of digital techno-logy and author of, among other titles, *The Internet Is Not the Answer* and *How to Fix the Future: Staying Human in the Digital Age*.

ALEXANDER LEE is a Research Fellow at the University of Warwick and the author of *Machiavelli: His Life and Times*.

CHRISTOPHER MORAN is an Associate Professor of US National Security in the Department of Politics and International Studies at the University of Warwick.

DANIEL T. POTTS is Professor of Ancient Near Eastern Archaeology and History at the Institute for the Study of the Ancient World, New York University. He is the founding editor-in-chief of the journal *Arabian Archaeology and Epigraphy* and a Corresponding Member of the German Archaeological Institute. He is the editor of the *Blackwell Companion to the Archaeology of the Ancient Near East* and the *Oxford Handbook of Iranian Archaeology*. His books include *Mesopotamia, Iran and Arabia from the Seleucids to the Sasanians*, *In the Land of the Emirates: The Archaeology and History of the UAE* and *Nomadism in Iran: From Antiquity to the Modern Era*.

SUZANNE RAINE is an Affiliate Lecturer at the Centre for Geopolitics, the University of Cambridge, a Visiting Professor at King's College London, and a Trustee at the Royal United Services Institute. Before that she worked in the British Foreign and Commonwealth Office, primarily on issues of national security and counter-terrorism.

JOSHUA ROVNER is a political scientist specialising in intelligence, strategy, and US foreign policy. Rovner is the co-editor of *Chaos in the Liberal Order: The Trump Presidency and International Politics in the Twenty-First Century*, which brings together leading historians, political scientists, and policy-makers to shed light on an extraordinary moment in world affairs. His first book was *Fixing the Facts: National Security and the Politics of Intelligence*, which won the International Studies Association's best book award for security studies, and the Edgar S. Furniss Book Award. In addition to his academic writing, he writes a monthly column for *War on the Rocks*. Professor Rovner is managing editor of H-Diplo's International Security Studies Forum and deputy editor of the *Journal of Strategic Studies*. He previously taught at the Southern Methodist University in Texas, the US Naval War College, and Columbia University. In 2018 and 2019 he served as scholar-in-residence at the National Security Agency and US Cyber Command.

NICK SPENCER is Senior Fellow at Theos and host of the *Reading Our Times* podcast.

BRENDAN SIMMS is director of the Centre for Geopolitics, University of Cambridge and the author of several works on European geopolitics.

CONSTANCE SIMMS read Modern Languages at the University of Oxford.

SIR HEW STRACHAN, FBA, FRSE, has been Wardlaw Professor of International Relations at the University of St Andrews since 2015. He is a Life Fellow of Corpus Christi College, Cambridge, where he was successively a Research Fellow and Fellow from 1975 to 1992, and an Emeritus Fellow of All Souls College, Oxford. His recent publications include *The First World War: To Arms*, *The First World War: A New Illustrated History* (based on his ten-part series for Channel 4) and *The Direction of War: Contemporary Strategy in Historical Perspective*.

HELEN THOMPSON is Professor of Political Economy at the University of Cambridge. She contributes a fortnightly column to the *New Statesman*.

SHARON WEINBERGER is a journalist and author of *The Imagineers of War: The Untold Story of DARPA, the Pentagon Agency that Changed the World*. She has written on military science and technology for the *New York Times*, the *Washington Post*, *Foreign Policy Magazine*, the *Financial Times* and many other publications, and has held fellowships at the Radcliffe Institute for Advanced Study at Harvard University among others.

ANDREW WILTON was formerly Keeper of British Art at the Tate Gallery and subsequently Visiting Research Fellow at Tate Britain. He retired in 2002, and is now Hon. Curator of Prints and Drawings at The Royal Academy and Hon. Curator of the Painter-Stainers' Company. His most recent books have been *Turner as Draughtsman* and *Frederic Church and the Landscape Oil Sketch*. A novel about Turner, *The Painter's Boy: An Historical Caprice*, appeared in 2019.

Image Rights ©

MAN AND TECHNOLOGY
How Humanity Thrives in a Changing World

Published by Bokförlaget Stolpe, Stockholm, Sweden, 2022

© The authors and Bokförlaget Stolpe 2022,
in association with the Axel and Margaret Ax:son Johnson Foundation for Public Benefit

The essays were commissioned by the Engelsberg Ideas editorial team.

Edited by
Kurt Almqvist, President, Axel and Margaret Ax:son Johnson Foundation
Alastair Benn, deputy editor, Engelsberg Ideas
Mattias Hessérus, project manager, Axel and Margaret Ax:son Johnson Foundation

Translation of Kurt Almqvist's introduction: Ruth Urbom
Text editor: Andrew Mackenzie
Design: Patric Leo
Layout: Petra Ahston Inkapööl
Cover image: Drawing for the silent film *Metropolis*, Otto Hunte, 1929
Pre-press and print coordinator: Italgraf Media AB, Sweden
Print: Printon, Estonia, via Italgraf Media, 2022
First edition, first printing

ISBN: 978-91-89425-89-7

BOKFÖRLAGET STOLPE

AXEL AND MARGARET AX:SON JOHNSON
FOUNDATION FOR PUBLIC BENEFIT